D0394847

AMERICAN NUREMBERG

AMERICAN NUREMBERG

The US Officials Who Should Stand Trial for Post-9/11 War Crimes

REBECCA GORDON

HOT BOOKS

Hot Books may be purchased in bulk at special discounts for sales promotion, corporate gifts, fund-raising, or educational purposes. Special editions can also be created to specifications. For details, contact the Special Sales Department, Skyhorse Publishing, 307 West 36th Street, 11th Floor, New York, NY 10018 or info@skyhorsepublishing.com.

Hot Books® and Skyhorse Publishing® are registered trademarks of Skyhorse Publishing, Inc.®, a Delaware corporation.

Visit our website at www.hotbookspress.com

10 9 8 7 6 5 4 3 2 1

Library of Congress Cataloging-in-Publication Data is available on file.

Cover design by Brian Peterson

ISBN: 978-1-5107-0333-9
Ebook ISBN: 978-1-5107-0338-4

Printed in the United States of America

Contents

To the victims and survivors
of the US war on terror

Acknowledgments

Many people have helped make this book possible. Perhaps my greatest debt—and that of the country—is to the journalists and researchers who have insisted on bringing the truth to light, even when it seemed no one wanted to look at it. Without their work we would not possess even the partial record we have today of the crimes committed in the war on terror. There are far too many to name them all, but any such list must include Andy Worthington, Jane Mayer, Seymour Hersh, and Jeremy Scahill.

I am especially grateful to several legal scholars who generously reviewed my drafts, reassured me that I was on the right track, and gave me their expert help in getting right the distinctions between the laws of war and human rights law. Any errors that remain in this text are mine alone. These scholars include Jameel Jaffer, Deputy Legal Director of the American Civil Liberties Union (ACLU); Sumner Twiss,

Florida State University's Distinguished Professor of Human Rights, Ethics, and Religion; and Almudena Bernabeu, Transitional Justice Program Director at the Center for Justice and Accountability (CJA). Almudena especially confirmed my belief that the first essential step in achieving justice for victims of human rights crimes is the public acknowledgement that these crimes have been committed. CJA, together with the ACLU and the Center for Constitutional Rights, are among the most important legal organizations working for the rights of detainees and for accountability for their torturers.

It was David Talbot of Hot Books who brought me this project and convinced me I was the right person to take it on. Thank you, David, for your faith in me, your thoughtful editing, and your vision for this book.

Thanks also go to Jim O'Brien, friend and indexer extraordinaire.

Finally, I am beyond grateful for the love and support of my most faithful reader and most honest critic, my partner Jan Adams.

Foreword

When Hot Books editorial director David Talbot first approached me about this project, I agreed that it needed to be done. Terrible crimes have been committed in the war on terror. They must be named, and those responsible must be held accountable.

But the proposed title made me very uncomfortable. Like many children of the 1950s and '60s, I grew up in the shadow of the Holocaust. Even on the day before he died, my Jewish father refused to tell me what kind of work he had done during the war for the Office of Strategic Services (OSS), the forerunner of the CIA. "I swore an oath," he said. In college, I took a semester of German. "I don't even want to hear those sounds come out of your mouth," he said. He never forgave Hannah Arendt for attempting to understand the Nazi mentality in *Eichmann in Jerusalem,* or the ACLU for helping American Nazis to march in Skokie, Illinois.

I grew up in a country still trying to assimilate the absolute barbarism of the Second World War. Adults around me were struggling to comprehend the feast of self-devouring horror served up by Europe, a continent that only decades before had so smugly shouldered the White Man's burden of civilizing the world. As was true for many Americans of my generation, Nazi Germany became my symbol and shorthand for human evil. And not without reason. The war the Nazis unleashed consumed the lives of between forty-five and fifty-five million Europeans, and another twenty-five to thirty million people in Asia. Twenty-seven million died in the Soviet Union, over fourteen percent of the total population; six million in Poland, seventeen percent of that population.*

When I was very young, my parents tried to shield me from the worst of the Holocaust. It would be years before I saw the photographs of those skeletal ghosts, before I understood my schoolmates' jokes about soap and lampshades. But I grew up knowing that the heart of darkness lay in Nazi Germany. The corollary, of course, was that my own country, which had fought the Nazis, was a light to the nations, a beacon of righteousness. When the war was over, my country had helped put the Nazis on trial as they deserved. We did it not because we were the winners and *could* do it, but because we were the wise and the good, and we knew that we *should* do it.

Because my parents were leftists, however, they wouldn't let me rest in my comfortable bed of American self-righteousness. They gave me another symbol for evil, another

---

* The United States lost 419,000, less than one-third of one percent of its population. If the Second World War had a winner, it was without doubt the United States of America.

bit of shorthand. My mother told me about the atomic bombs my country dropped first on Hiroshima, and then a few days later—just to make sure the Japanese (and the Soviets) understood what they were facing—on Nagasaki. Later I would learn about the Allies' crimes: the destruction of German cities like Dresden with firebombs that did more damage and killed more civilians than the German air war on England. I would learn about how, near the end of the war, the United States leveled sixty-seven Japanese cities with incendiary bombs that killed half a million residents outright and burned to ashes the homes of five million more. War crimes, all.

Facing these monumental horrors of the past, I was not thrilled with the title "American Nuremberg." Compared with the unimaginable scale of World War II—including the genocidal Final Solution, the Allied firebombing of Europe and Japan, and the radioactive ruins of Hiroshima and Nagasaki—the crimes of the war on terror seem to be of a much smaller order.

But I have come to appreciate the title of this book and the frame it has offered for this project. US crimes in the war on terror matter. They matter because hundreds of thousands have died, millions have been made homeless, an unknown number have been kidnapped, tortured, and disappeared— and because the nation responsible for all this is the most powerful the world has ever known. These crimes matter because impunity is a dangerous thing, both for the souls of the people of this still nominally democratic country, and for the rest of the world, which has to live with us.

There were a few at Nuremberg, like the British journalist Peter Calvocoressi, who hoped and believed that once the Allies were done bringing the Nazi leaders to justice, they

Introduction

The modern concept of human rights is based on the fundamental principle that those responsible for violations must be held to account.

—Ben Emmerson, UN Special Rapporteur
on Counter-Terrorism and Human Rights

Well, when the president does it, that means it is not illegal.

—Richard Nixon, in 1977
interview with David Frost

September 11, 2001, began an ominous new chapter in this country's history. Horrified Americans turned our eyes from the images on TV screens and toward our government. We were looking for reassurance, for bold actions to assuage our newfound fears. And the government responded.

First, President George W. Bush told us to go shopping. All over the country businesses began displaying posters bearing an image of the Stars and Stripes that had sprouted handles. The American flag had become a shopping bag, accompanied by a patriotic new slogan: "America: Open for Business." In a moment of high national unity, we watched a New York City firefighter ring the bell to reopen the stock exchange on Wall Street.

Then the serious response began as the president proclaimed a "war on terror" and unleashed the full might of US military and security forces. Bush announced the establishment of a new, Cabinet-level Department of Homeland Security and, within a couple of months, Congress passed the USA Patriot Act, granting the federal government unprecedented secret surveillance and subpoena powers. Soon, ordinary Americans became accustomed to the rituals of the new security regime every time we went to the airport or stood in line for a ball game.

In San Francisco, where I live, residents and tourists watched as National Guard troops began patrolling the Golden Gate Bridge, distinctly visible in their camouflaged troop carriers. Visitors to corporate towers and federal buildings across the country were not surprised to see armed guards staring menacingly at them, and moviegoers across the country were warned over public address systems to report any suspicious activity. Uniformed soldiers carrying automatic weapons became a common sight at airports. My partner and I suddenly found ourselves on an FBI "No-Fly" list, most likely because we were among the founders of *War Times/Tiempo de guerras,* a free, nationally distributed, bi-lingual tabloid opposing this new, all-encompassing "war." And we all got used to seeing the color-coded warnings of the official danger gauge known as the Terrorist Threat Level.

We also began to get used to the idea that keeping us safe would require, as Vice President Dick Cheney put it, "working the dark side." There were no real objections when Cofer Black, director of the CIA's Counterterrorism Center, told Congress, "After September 11, the gloves come off." Did we even blink when, on November 5, 2001, *Newsweek*'s liberal pundit Jonathan Alter wrote that it was "Time to think about torture"? There were a few cautionary remarks from people who cared about civil liberties. But eventually, most of us settled back into a new and extraordinary normal.

Meanwhile, behind the scenes, the war on terror was just getting started. By September 12, Vice President Cheney was already working on efforts to pin the 9/11 attacks on Saddam Hussein. By January 2002, the prison camp at Guantánamo Bay was established. By late 2002, those who wanted to could read stories of CIA kidnapping ("extraordinary rendition") and torture ("stress and duress") in the pages of the *Washington Post* or the *New York Times*. Soon after came the revelations of abuses at Abu Ghraib, Bagram Air Force Base, and dozens of CIA "dark sites" around the world. Then we heard about the "ghost prisoners" who died in US custody, about waterboarding, "rectal rehydration," and mock executions. We heard about the people, including US citizens, assassinated on foreign soil by rockets fired from drone aircraft controlled by young American "pilots" sitting half a world away in the Nevada desert.

To this day, the people of the United States have never had a full accounting of all that has been done in our name as part of an apparently endless war on terror. After years of struggle, we finally have the heavily redacted 500-page executive summary of the Senate Intelligence Committee's 6,000-page report on the torture allowed by the CIA. But it contains only a partial accounting of the actions of a single US agency among the many security branches involved in the war on terror.*

Nor has there been any real public reckoning for those officials, including men (and a few women) at the highest levels of the government who are responsible for all these deeply troubling actions undertaken by Washington since 9/11. This impunity all but guarantees that the next time our country is seized by a spasm of fear, we can expect more crimes committed in the name of national, and our own, security.

Indeed, as I finished writing this book, Paris was struck by a night of terror which left at least 130 people dead—and which, all too predictably, triggered a wave of overheated political rhetoric and calls for even more extreme security measures. In the United States, half of all state governors leapt to declare that their states would not accept any of the modest number of Syrian refugees scheduled for entry to the US— refugees who were made homeless by a civil war that our own government helped to start. Meanwhile, the two leading candidates for the 2016 Republican presidential nomination competed to see who could be the mostly vehemently intolerant and authoritarian, with Donald Trump flatly declaring that the US should shut its doors to all Syrian refugees, even women and infants, and calling for the creation of a "registry" for all Muslims in America. At the same time, Ben Carson, another leading GOP contender, compared Syrian refugees to "rabid dogs" that should be kept safely outside our borders.

---

* Many observers have pointed out the absurdity of declaring war either on a tactic (terrorism) or on an emotion (terror). A crusade against terror seems even more ill-defined and hopeless than the US "war" on drugs. For simplicity's sake, I will not qualify the "war on terror" with quote marks throughout this book. But they remain present in my mind's eye, and I hope in the reader's as well.

Why "Nuremberg"?

Between November 1945 and April 1949, the four countries known as the Great Powers—the United States, the Soviet Union, Great Britain, and France—tried nearly 200 Nazi war criminals at Nuremberg, Germany. Hundreds more were later put on trial in Soviet-occupied countries and in West German courts. But the tribunal that fixed itself most deeply in the public imagination was the first, nearly year-long Nuremberg trial—from November 20, 1945 to October 1, 1946—during which twenty-two major Nazi officials stood accused of responsibility for the Nazi war machine's aggression against other countries and the Third Reich's eliminationist policies directed against the Jewish people and other targeted populations. Adolf Hitler himself escaped justice at Nuremberg by committing suicide in the final days of the war, as did such top aides as SS chief Heinrich Himmler, head of Hitler's extermination program, and Joseph Goebbels, the Third Reich's master propagandist. But the men who did stand trial during the first Nuremberg tribunal represented an important spectrum of Nazi power, including Hitler's second-in-command, Reich Marshal Hermann Goering.

The series of trials at Nuremberg remain controversial to this day, with scholars and legal experts debating whether justice was done. Now, as they did then, some scholars question the tribunal's legal foundations. Others believe that too many Nazis avoided prosecution, pointing to defendants who were acquitted on dubious grounds or were later reprieved. And there were many Nazis who escaped the tribunals altogether, often with the assistance of US officials eager to recruit them for the Cold War effort against Russia. (Adolf Eichmann was one of the few who was later tracked down, in his case by

Israeli agents who kidnapped him in Argentina and brought him to Israel to stand trial.)

But despite the ongoing debate over either the tribunal's legality or the effectiveness of international law in the face of World War II's staggering crimes against humanity, it is widely believed that some kind of justice was done at Nuremberg. The very name, for many, conjures a deeply righteous legal and moral reckoning that, by grappling with the unspeakable outrages of the Third Reich, allowed humanity to go forward.

In 1945 the victorious Allies could very well have simply executed captured Nazi leaders. In fact, that's what President Franklin Roosevelt and British Prime Minister Winston Churchill originally proposed doing. (Churchill thought that somewhere between fifty to one hundred top Nazi officials should be summarily put to death.) This would have saved the Allies the mess, expense, and public scrutiny involved in holding trials. Ironically, it was Soviet dictator Joseph Stalin who insisted on trials for accused Nazi war criminals, arguing that such procedures were necessary to establish a sense of legitimacy in the eyes of the world. So the allied nations—the United States, the United Kingdom, France, and the Soviet Union—took the legal route to justice.

As we shall see in Chapter 1, the resultant tribunals were far from perfect, but they accomplished several things. They forced a public, international acknowledgement of the scale of Nazi crimes (while also obscuring the winning side's war crimes). They brought a modicum of due process to the prosecutions. But perhaps most important of all, the tribunals demonstrated the crucial importance of international law. By construing Nazi depredations as *crimes* rather than as simple acts of a war that Germany had lost, the tribunals demonstrated that international law—specifically the laws and customs of war—is *real law*. And, just as with domestic crime, international crime can have real consequences.

The Allies had substantial incentive to shore up the power and reach of international law. Europe had barely survived its second catastrophic world war in three decades. With the United States and the Soviet Union already circling each other, Europe was desperate to avoid another such cataclysm. The last one had killed upwards of fifty-five million Europeans and had left the lands and economies of victors and losers alike in ruins. And the United States had just demonstrated in Hiroshima and Nagasaki that it commanded the most powerful weapon the world had ever seen. It was possible now to imagine a war that would annihilate all of humanity.

This was the shadow that loomed over Nuremberg as the tribunals began. Together with the charters founding the United Nations and the International Court of Justice—as well as the revised Geneva Conventions of 1949—the Nuremberg trials would seek to substitute the rule of law for the rule of force. Imperfect instruments constructed by imperfect beings, these international advances nonetheless established the possibility that conflicts between nations could—and should—be conducted according to agreed-upon laws. These treaties and charters, and the ones that have followed them, are a zenith in human political achievement. They are among the few positive results of the Second World War.

International law is even more important in 2016 than it was in 1945. There are now nine nuclear-armed states.* Any

---

* Of these, six have signed the Nuclear Nonproliferation Treaty, but only five admit to possessing nuclear weapons: China, France, Russia, Britain and United States. Israel also signed the NPT, but has never publicly acknowledged its nuclear arsenal. Three nuclear-armed countries have not signed: India, Pakistan, and North Korea.

one of them could start a species-ending war. In the meantime, conventional wars and intra-national armed conflicts continue to ravage the planet. Combined with long-term climate change and growing resource shortages, they have produced a human migration crisis in the Mediterranean. But despite the increasingly urgent need for the international rule of law, the United States continues to behave as if such laws are only, as the notorious hotelier Leona Helmsley once said about taxes, "for the little people."

That is why this book is called *American Nuremberg*. There is a pressing need to bring the United States into the legal community of nations, where it must be held accountable for its actions. Let us be clear: the scale of US crimes in the war on terror comes nowhere near the genocidal war-making of the Nazis. But ever since World War II, the American empire has put its heavy boots on every continent. Even in imperial decline—after disastrous wars in Vietnam, Afghanistan, and Iraq, and facing long-term challenges from China and Russia—it remains the world's preeminent military and economic power. If the most powerful country in the world—a country that still, decades after the end of the Soviet Union, calls itself "the leader of the free world"—can violate international laws of war and human rights with complete impunity, then why should any other nation be constrained? For the sake of the victims of the war on terror, for the sake of our national soul, but even more for the future of humanity, we need a full accounting and real accountability for American war criminals. We need an American Nuremberg.

Organizing the Prosecution

The organizers of the original Nuremberg tribunal faced a serious conceptual problem when deciding whom to charge and how. Had they sought to prosecute each significant Nazi official and military officer for every individual breach of international and domestic law, the tribunal might well have lasted late into the 20th century. The Allies had to find a way to categorize the most heinous of the crimes: the deportations and exterminations of entire populations; the murders of hundreds of thousands of enslaved laborers worked to death in German factories; and the deaths of millions of combatants and civilians in an unprovoked war of aggression. They had to consider thousands of individual actions (attested to in a million pages of documentary evidence) and corral them into a few conceptual pens. They chose three main categories for their indictments: crimes against peace, war crimes, and crimes against humanity.

Like the crimes prosecuted at Nuremberg, those committed during the US war on terror are so numerous, so vile, and so varied that it is no simple matter to describe them in an orderly way. Which of George W. Bush's and Dick Cheney's actions can we call war crimes? Which are crimes against peace? Do any of them amount to crimes against humanity? How do we define the crimes of psychologists Bruce Jessen and James Mitchell, the highly-paid consultants who helped design the CIA's torture program? What crimes, if any, were committed by Justice Department attorneys Jay Bybee and John Yoo, authors of the infamous "torture memos"? What about Secretary of Defense Donald Rumsfeld, with his airy dismissal ("stuff happens") of the violent anarchy that his invasion of Iraq unleashed on the people of that country? In hopes of bringing some kind of order to this ethical and legal snarl, I've chosen to organize US crimes in the war on terror into three main categories: crimes against peace, war crimes, and human rights crimes.

Using the term "war crimes" in the context of the war on terror is somewhat problematic. The suggestion that US officials might be guilty of war crimes implies that the "war on terror" is a real war. For reasons that will become clear, however, I've chosen to call only those crimes against individuals that have taken place inside the war zones of Afghanistan and Iraq *war crimes*. The extreme security measures that the US has undertaken in other areas—including tortures, extraordinary renditions and targeted killings—are *human rights crimes*.

Why not use the category of "crimes against humanity," as the Allies did at Nuremberg? Certainly the global war on terror has seen violently inhumane actions. The CIA employed "rectal rehydration" to punish Khalid Sheikh Mohammed and to demonstrate their "total control over" him. The Defense Department sent Mohamedou Ould Slahi blindfolded out on a boat on Guantánamo Bay to have his clothes stuffed full of ice cubes and to be beaten for hours. Then they shoved him into a specially prepared trailer, sealed to prevent any light from entering, fitted with loudspeakers and a single ring bolted in the middle of the concrete floor, where he remained for months. The US Navy held José Padilla without charge in isolation for years in a brig in Charleston, South Carolina, subjecting him to brutal tortures, including sensory and sleep deprivation, excruciating stress positions, and, according to his lawyers, administration of a "truth serum." When finally brought to trial, Padilla was deemed psychologically incapable of assisting his attorneys in his own defense because his trauma far exceeded ordinary PTSD. Years of torture on US soil had rendered him psychotic. In the hysterical climate of the post-9/11 United States, US authorities mentally dismantled an American citizen who had virtually no legal protections.

Surely these must be crimes against humanity? They are certainly horrific violations of human persons, but in a strict legal sense they are probably not crimes against humanity. In international law that term is reserved for a very specific kind of crime—the widespread or systematic targeting of an entire people, religion, or political group for persecution and/or extermination. Awful as the crimes against Mohammed, Slahi, Padilla, and many others are, they probably do not rise to the level of crimes against humanity. That is why I've chosen to call them human rights crimes.

Suppose our own alleged criminals in the war on terror were to be brought to justice. Who could try them? In what venue? The United States signed but never ratified the treaty creating the International Criminal Court (ICC). In fact, in 2002 the Bush administration informed the United Nations that the country had no interest in pursuing ratification—so the ICC is not an option. Some countries have anti-torture and war crimes laws, so US government officials accused of these crimes might in theory be tried in Spain, or even Switzerland, should they happen to visit such foreign nations. But even if one or two accused were to be unexpectedly hauled before a judge on foreign soil, such trials would still fall short of holding accountable all of those who in Latin America are called the "intellectual authors" of such crimes.

That leaves the problem in *our* hands, the hands of the people of the world and especially the people of this country. It is up to us to bring our criminals to some sort of justice, even if it is unofficial. This book is a modest step in that direction.

The first chapter describes the original Nuremberg tribunal, and the second lays the legal groundwork for an American Nuremberg. Chapters 3, 4, and 5 each treat one of the three broad kinds of criminal behavior—crimes against peace, war crimes, and human rights crimes—and name those individuals who I believe should face justice. In the conclusion I briefly propose a model for an American Nuremberg tribunal.

Failing that grand reckoning, there are a few intermediate steps the United States might take in order to, as a friend and expert in international human rights law suggested to me, demonstrate that the United States has begun a process of political maturation. It would certainly be a good thing if this country could stop behaving like an angry two-year-old child, stomping around the world waving drone missiles and smashing things with our outsized feet. In the book's conclusion, I will present five concrete steps the United States ought to take immediately. Recognizing that each of these requires a political will that is not present in today's political climate, I conclude with another suggested action—the convening of an unofficial, but highly legitimate public tribunal.

As I write these words, many white people in my country are in the midst of awakening to a reality that communities of color have long known in their bones: police forces in the United States can capture, detain without charge, torture, and kill people of color with almost complete impunity. I cannot help but see the parallels between coercive policing at home and the coercion of detention, torture, and illegal killing in the world at large. In both cases, the victims are often poor and almost always people of color. In both cases, the fact that the perpetrators receive no public censure and suffer no personal consequences makes these practices normal and normative. It takes a major change in social thinking to recognize them for what they really are: officially sanctioned criminal acts.

But people can make that effort. The activists of Black Lives Matter have finally pushed the old news of institutionalized police violence onto front pages. Years of legal scholarship by groundbreaking intellectuals like Michelle Alexander and grassroots organizing work may yet remove the scourge of mass incarceration and police terror borne by the poor and minorities in this country. In the same way, Americans can also make the effort to shift our perspective and recognize the crimes of our national officials in the war on terror. The world is waiting for us.

Chapter 1

The First Nuremberg

We must not forget that the record on which we judge
the defendants today is the record on which we will be
judged tomorrow.

—Robert H. Jackson, Associate Justice
of the US Supreme Court and chief prosecutor
for the United States at Nuremberg

The first Nuremberg trial occupied eleven months
between 1945 and 1946. Confronting the evidence
of barbarism on a scale unknown in human history,
World War II's victors sought a way to bring accountability to
perpetrators and justice to victims. The question they faced
was how this could be done so that the world would understand their actions as a genuine attempt at justice rather than
a masquerade of vengeance. They sought to demonstrate
that their justice had a basis in international law, and in the
process they consolidated and advanced the very idea of

international law—a concept that seemed all the more necessary to human life in a postwar world of atomic weapons and US–Soviet conflict. Seventy years on, the international community for the most part recognizes the Nuremberg tribunal as a legitimate forum in which justice, however imperfectly, was done.

The twenty-two defendants in the dock for the opening round of Nuremberg trials included former high government officials, military officers, and propagandists in the Nazi regime, as well as the banker who masterminded the rise of Hitler's war machine. The process drew on some of the best legal minds in the four allied nations conducting the tribunal. Its foundations and procedures, enshrined in historic formal agreements, set the precedent for all subsequent international attempts to bring war criminals to justice. Today's International Tribunal for Yugoslavia and the International Tribunal for Rwanda, for example, are both modeled on Nuremberg.

In addition to the twenty-two verdicts rendered, Nuremberg had other enduring results. Among these are the 1950 Nuremberg Principles. These guiding rules for nations, commissioned in 1947 by the UN General Assembly, remain valuable today as a means of judging the actions of governments and their officials. They create a useful lens for examining the actions of US officials in the war on terror. The Nuremberg Principles declare that actions that violate international law are punishable crimes, regardless of whether those actions happen to violate domestic laws. Even heads of state or other high government officials are not immune from prosecution for war crimes and crimes against humanity. And no one can be exonerated for war crimes or crimes against humanity on the sole grounds that he or she was acting under a superior's orders.

These principles continue to guide the work of the International Criminal Court today. The ICC is itself an outgrowth of the Nuremberg process. Even during the opening Nuremberg trial, observers expected that the United Nations would establish such a court as one of its earliest actions; in the end it took more than half a century to achieve this. However, by 1998, sixty countries had approved the ICC's governing document, the Rome Statute.* The international court itself finally opened in 2002, and by 2015, 123 countries had signed on. Conspicuous by its absence is the United States of America.

The Nuremberg trials were the result of heated political discussions within Allied circles dating back to 1943. At a conference of Allies held in Tehran during the war, Joseph Stalin is said to have raised a toast to the prospect of quickly trying and then shooting 50,000 Nazi war criminals. Winston Churchill was reportedly horrified, and apparently Roosevelt made an attempt to reduce the tension in the room by joking that perhaps the Allies could make do with only shooting 49,000. While some Allied nations warned at a 1943 conference in Moscow that Nazi war criminals would be pursued "to the uttermost ends of the earth . . . in order that justice be done," some elements within the British and American governments were strongly resistant to the idea.

This opposition to a war crimes tribunal was especially strong in the US State Department, where an elite old-boy network with reflexive anti-Semitic attitudes held sway. Looking beyond the present war to the next, albeit "cold," one these government officials were as concerned about restoring German strength as a bulwark against the Soviet

---

* The ICC is not part of the United Nations. It is an independent organization, established through the Rome Statute.

Union after the war as they were about bringing Nazi criminals to justice. Beyond the issue of future Soviet power, there were immediate issues to consider as well. US Secretary of the Treasury Henry Morgenthau, Jr., believed that it would be both risky and wrong to give Nazis like Hermann Goering the kind of propaganda platform a public trial would afford. Others, including Henry Stimson, Roosevelt's Secretary of War, argued that only a public trial bearing the imprimatur of the international community would satisfy both the practical need to discredit Nazi Germany in the world's eyes and the moral requirements of justice.

The Nuremberg tribunal was by no means Europe's first war crimes trial. Private individuals had been tried for crimes committed during previous European wars. Usually the defendants were soldiers, often enlisted men, accused of abusing prisoners of war or civilians in the course of their service. These defendants were tried either in the civilian courts of the country of the victims or, more often, in military tribunals held in their own countries. In any case, these trials were always local. They relied on domestic civilian or military laws and were specific to individuals and their individual offenses.

Peter Calvocoressi, a British intelligence officer seconded to the prosecuting team at Nuremberg, described two key problems the tribunal's organizers faced in a commentary published in 1947. "In the first place," he wrote, "there were men whom the Allies wished to accuse but whose alleged crimes related to no particular country and were confined to no particular point of time." The Nazi government's crimes had covered an entire continent. It made no practical sense, for example, to try the same men three times in three venues for the slaughter of Jews in Germany, France, and Poland.

Second, merely punishing lower-echelon soldiers for "exceeding their rights and their instructions" was "plainly inadequate for the punishment of War Crimes as extended by the practices of war in the present century." The problem was not simply "that of indicting a disobedient subordinate in the field whose temperament had led him to commit some hot-blooded excess." The problem was finding a way to try the people who had put those soldiers in the field in the first place, to get at the "directing hand in high places," the hand that had instituted "a deliberate criminal policy which was responsible for the cold-blooded devising of excesses."

One option was to allow what remained of the German state try its own war criminals. This is what the Allies had done at the end of World War I. Quite a few lower-echelon Germans were tried in German courts at Leipzig between 1921 and 1927, but few were convicted and even fewer punished. This time, however, the Allies were not content to leave the prosecution of war crimes in German hands. If trials were to be held, it was clear that no single country could hold them. They must have an international character, ideally under the aegis of a body like the newly formed United Nations, which was established in October 1945, a month before the first Nuremberg trial began. And the trials must find a way to apply the rule of law not only to the soldiers in the field but to the "directing hands" that had put them there.

The Nuremberg court was established in August 1945 through a joint document known as the London Agreement, signed by representatives of each of the four Great Powers. Article 1 stated:

> There shall be established after consultation with the Control Council for Germany an International Military Tribunal for the trial of war criminals whose

offenses have no particular geographical location whether they be accused individually or in their capacity as members of the organizations or groups or in both capacities.

How the tribunal was to function and the specific crimes it would consider were established in the Charter of the International Military Tribunal (also called the London Charter), which formed part of the entire agreement. Each of the four Great Powers was to provide one judge and one alternate, all of whom were to be present for all sessions. Each country also supplied a chief prosecutor, all four of whom were to work together to organize their case. The prosecutors were also to draft procedures for the trial, which they then submitted to the full tribunal for approval. The accused were to be defended by attorneys of their own choosing.

Jurisdiction and Specific Crimes

Article 6 of the charter defined the Nuremberg tribunal's purpose and jurisdiction. The tribunal existed to facilitate "the trial and punishment of the major war criminals of the European Axis countries." Its powers were those of trying and punishing "persons who, acting in the interests of the European Axis countries, whether as individuals or as members of organizations, committed any" of three broad types of crime:

(a) CRIMES AGAINST PEACE: namely, planning, preparation, initiation or waging of a war of aggression, or a war in violation of international treaties, agreements or assurances, or participation in a common plan or conspiracy for the accomplishment of any of the foregoing;

(b) WAR CRIMES: namely, violations of the laws or customs of war. Such violations shall include, but not be limited to, murder, ill-treatment or deportation to slave labor or for any other purpose of civilian population of or in occupied territory, murder or ill-treatment of prisoners of war or persons on the seas, killing of hostages, plunder of public or private property, wanton destruction of cities, towns or villages, or devastation not justified by military necessity;

(c) CRIMES AGAINST HUMANITY: namely, murder, extermination, enslavement, deportation, and other inhumane acts committed against any civilian population, before or during the war; or persecutions on political, racial or religious grounds in execution of or in connection with any crime within the jurisdiction of the Tribunal, whether or not in violation of the domestic law of the country where perpetrated.

The first and last of these three categories of crime were innovations in international law. During the four-party negotiations that established the Nuremberg tribunal and its rules, the United States also insisted on including the crime of "waging a war of aggression"—a crime against peace— and on placing it at the head of the list. Associate Supreme Court Justice Robert H. Jackson, who served as chief negotiator for the United States and later as its chief prosecutor at Nuremberg, argued that by starting an unprovoked war, Germany had violated international laws and treaties, specifically the 1928 Kellogg–Briand Pact. The US position, also supported by Roosevelt's Secretary of War Henry Stimson, was that all the rest of Germany's war crimes sprang from this first crime against peace.

The Kellogg–Briand Pact, made in the years between the two world wars, was an international agreement to renounce war as a means of settling conflicts between nations. "Individuals who violate this Pact by launching an aggressive war commit no less criminal act than do individuals who violate the Hague and Geneva Conventions by murdering prisoners of war," said Stimson. "They simply do it on a greater and more destructive scale."

The French and Russians were less supportive of the crimes against peace charge. They, and later critics, argued that it was unjust to try the Nazis *ex post facto* for a crime that appeared on no nation's law books at the start of the war. In his sweeping history *The Anatomy of the Nuremberg Trials,* Telford Taylor acknowledged that "crimes against peace" would not have passed legal muster if the trial had been "conducted on a plane devoid of political and emotional factors." Taylor, who replaced Jackson as US prosecutor for the twelve subsequent Nuremberg trials of lower-level functionaries, believes that trying the Germans for starting the war violated the common law principle (also enshrined in Article I of the US Constitution) that no one should be tried for *ex post facto* crimes. However, in 1945 those "political and emotional factors" were crucially important if the Nuremberg tribunal was to serve its purpose. "Peoples whose nations had been attacked and dismembered without warning," Taylor argues, "wanted legal retribution, whether or not this was a 'first time.'"

Although contentious, the idea that military aggression is itself a crime was not a new one. In fact, the founder of international law, the 17th century legal scholar Hugo Grotius, recognized aggression in his work on the laws of war, *De jure belli ac pacis*. But no nation and no person had ever been tried for such a crime before.

The Nazis' attempt to exterminate entire peoples (Jews, the Romany), or entire political and social groupings (communists, labor activists, gays, the physically and mentally impaired), also presented difficulties. What Hitler's regime had done was qualitatively different from the mere sum of millions of individual murders. These victims of the Third Reich were systematically collected and killed because of who they were. How to conceptualize this kind of crime, one that had never before been prosecuted? The Nuremberg tribunal fixed on a new name for this unprecedented horror: crimes against humanity, and defined them in connection with "any crime within the jurisdiction of the Tribunal." That phrase referred to the other two categories of crime, crimes against peace and war crimes. The 1950 Nuremberg Principles extended this definition beyond the temporal confines of the Second World War to include any such "persecutions" that are "carried on in execution of or in connection with any crime against peace or any war crime."

In 1948, two years after Nuremberg's conclusion, the new United Nations promulgated the world's first treaty defining the crime of genocide, which most nations have signed and ratified, including the United States. This treaty provided the legal basis for including genocide, in addition to crimes against humanity and violations of the 1949 Geneva Conventions, among the charges brought at the International Tribunals on Rwanda and the former Yugoslavia. The Yugoslavia tribunal also addressed "violations of the laws and customs of war," that vast body of common law and experience describing how war ought and ought not to be carried out.

Article 6 of the London Charter also identifies conspiracy, not as a separate category of crime, but as an additional consideration in relation to any of the three main categories. Conspiracy was included in order to establish the principle that not only the soldiers and other functionaries with bloody hands would be punished, but also those high officials who gave the orders, however clean their hands might appear. "Leaders, organizers, instigators and accomplices," Article 6 concluded, "participating in the formulation or execution of a common plan or conspiracy to commit any of the foregoing crimes are responsible for all acts performed by any persons in execution of such plan."

The potential charge of conspiracy also raised concerns about its legitimacy among Nuremberg prosecutors. While there was ample precedent for prosecuting criminal conspiracies such as racketeering in the United States, there was little in England and still less in continental Europe. Conspiracy is a problematic charge, both because it is difficult to prove and because it can be misused to create guilt by mere association with the wrong people or the wrong organization. On the other hand, the Nuremberg tribunal's framers needed some means of indicting not only those who ran the Nazi death camps, but also those who had put the whole machinery of murder in motion.

Critiques of Nuremberg

Over the years, Nuremberg has encountered its critics, whose critiques have mainly followed three lines of argument: that the trial represented victors' justice; that some defendants were tried for offenses that were not legally crimes at the time they were committed (and thus involved *ex post facto* laws); and that the Allies themselves had committed war crimes and so had no right to try others for the same offenses—the "*tu quoque*" argument ("you did it, too").

Was Nuremberg victors' justice? That is, was the trial nothing more than the vengeance of the winners masquerading as justice for the losers? There are arguments supporting this position. For example, the trials were not conducted according to common law rules of justice. Indeed, Article 19 of the London Charter stated, "The Tribunal shall not be bound by technical rules of evidence. It shall adopt and apply to the greatest possible extent expeditious and nontechnical procedure, and shall admit any evidence which it deems to be of probative value." In addition, defendants were often presented on the witness stand with documents that neither they nor their defense attorneys had seen before. This practice is contrary at least to US rules of discovery in criminal law, although the presiding justices at Nuremberg seemed to believe that surprising a defendant with documentation of his actions was a legitimate court tactic.*

The Nuremberg trials were the imperfect product of imperfect human beings, working from two very different conceptions of justice—English common law for the United States and the United Kingdom, and the Napoleonic Code for France and Russia. Nonetheless, there is significant evidence that they were to a large extent fair and legitimate trials. Not least is the fact that of the twenty-two men tried

---

* This is evident in the transcript of the questioning of Goering by US prosecutor (and Supreme Court Justice) Robert H. Jackson. In defense of the prosecution, they were still digging through more than a million pages of the Nazi regime's meticulous records, even as the trial proceeded. Documents had to be translated into English, which was not always done perfectly, and of course modern photocopying technology had yet to be invented.

during the first round, three—Hans Fritzsche, Franz von Papen, and Hjalmar Schacht—were acquitted. Furthermore, as Calvocoressi argued in 1947, the Great Powers could have taken as a given that war crimes had been committed, and then moved quickly to judge the accused. Instead, the Nuremberg prosecutors took the time and trouble to document the Nazi crimes in detail—a model that those hoping to prosecute contemporary US war criminals would do well to follow.

What about the charge that the Nuremberg defendants were tried according to *ex post facto* laws? Was military aggression actually a crime at the time the Nazis launched their war? As we noted above, many people, including US War Secretary Stimson were convinced then, and many are convinced today, that a war of aggression was a crime under unwritten-but-long-recognized customary law and specifically under the Kellogg–Briand Pact, which Germany had signed. Nuremberg simply marked the first international attempt to actually hold the leaders of a nation accountable for launching such a war.

Finally, did the Allies have the right to try German leaders when they themselves could also have been indicted for war crimes? Those who made this criticism had in mind such crimes as French mistreatment of German prisoners of war, the firebombing of German and Japanese cities (in which hundreds of thousands of civilians died),* and the US decision to drop atomic bombs on Hiroshima and Nagasaki. It was the hope of some observers at the time that when an International Court of Criminal Law was established, it would consider such horrors as the use of atomic weapons

---

* It is likely that guilt over Allied firebombing is one reason why German air attacks on English cities did not feature in the Nuremberg indictments.

on Japan as its first order of business. This, as we know, did not happen. But the question remained: did the crimes of the Allies render those of the Axis powers less horrific, less worthy of judgment?

I believe that the crimes of the Nazi regime were so vast, so heinous, and so unprecedented that they demanded an unprecedented international response. Only an international judicial reckoning could reestablish the place of justice in the affairs of humanity. This does not obviate the fact that certain actions by the US and its allies—including the fire-bombing of civilian populations and the atomic bombing of Hiroshima and Nagasaki—also cried out to be fully examined in an international court.

A similar question might be asked today. Do al Qaeda's crimes on 9/11 exonerate those responsible for the disappearance and torture of thousands in the war on terror, or indeed for the deaths of hundreds of thousands in the US war on Iraq? My answer is no. Certainly the 9/11 attacks were horrific criminal actions, as are the bombings of markets and mosques, the kidnappings and assassinations that terrorist networks continue to carry out today. But these crimes in no way justify the extraordinary and disproportionate storm of war, incarceration and torture that the United States has unleashed against populations in the Middle East, northern Africa, and Asia. Nor did these 9/11 assaults demand the broadly repressive measures that the US government took against its own people.

Some Final Comments

To read the record of the Nuremberg tribunal is to come face to face with human suffering and human criminality on a scale beyond imagining: the hundreds of thousands of disabled people murdered in the service of ethnic cleansing, in its original sense—the cleansing of the "Aryan" people of any stain of mental or physical disability; the million or more on all sides who died when enemy bombs incinerated their cities; the tens of millions gassed, shot, starved, and worked to death by the Nazi state; the equal numbers who died on battlefields or from war wounds. All told, somewhere between sixty-five and eighty million people are thought to have died in World War II. The dead stare out at us across the decades, and we wonder what kind of justice they received at Nuremberg.

Human beings can comprehend the suffering of others much better in the particular than in the aggregate. The recitation of the vast numbers of dead, wounded, and disappeared simply leaves one stunned.

We can, then, read about the fate of a man named Dilawar, a taxi driver from a small town in southern Afghanistan.* A local militia leader "sold" Dilawar to the US military in hopes of currying favor with the occupying forces. US soldiers chained him by his wrists to the ceiling of his cell for days and beat his legs so badly that when the guards tried to make him kneel, they would no longer bend. He died alone, chained in a standing position. A coroner who examined the autopsy report described the condition of his legs as "pulpified."

We can read about Dilawar and experience whatever reaction of horror or repugnance his story might prompt in us. But how can we understand a million Dilawars? Eighty million?

---

* Dilawar's story is recounted in the 2007 documentary film *Taxi to the Dark Side.*

What the United States has done in the course of the war on terror does not approach the statistical horrors of World War II. But that doesn't make the suffering any less for those whose family members have been blown up in a drone strike, or who have been "renditioned" to a black site, or been subjected to "enhanced interrogation," or have been forced by chaos and war to leave their homes forever. People do not suffer in the aggregate; they suffer as individuals. And when they suffer as the result of crimes committed by high officials of any nation, they deserve to have the truth told and the guilty held accountable. They deserve justice.

Chapter 2

Broken Treaties, Broken Laws

"I wished they had killed me," Khan told his lawyers. He said that he experienced excruciating pain when hung naked from poles and that guards repeatedly held his head under ice water.

— Reuters, June 2, 2015

When the CIA abducted Majid Khan in Pakistan in 2003; when agency personnel poured ice water on his genitals; when they immersed his whole body in ice water and held his head under until he almost drowned; when they "stripped him naked" and "hung him from a beam for three days;" when they shoved a tube up his rectum and used it to "feed" him his pureed lunch; when they kept him isolated in total darkness for almost a year; what crimes, if any, did they commit?

If the United States were to hold accountable American officials and torturers for crimes committed under the banner of the war on terror, under what laws—international and/or national—might they be tried?

The answers to this question depend in part on the extent to which the war on terror really is a *war*. There is a difference between acts of terrorism—which are atrocious and illegal under many domestic and international laws—and the kind of hostilities that international treaties like the Geneva Conventions call "armed conflict." Wars involve sustained levels of regular fighting. Unfortunately, neither the Geneva Conventions nor its Additional Protocols explicitly define an "armed conflict." This definition is important because it affects the kind of rights prisoners can claim.

Marco Sassòli, professor of international law at the University of Geneva in Switzerland, has written extensively on this question. In a 2006 article for Harvard University's Program on Humanitarian Policy and Conflict Research, he offered some criteria for recognizing an armed conflict. "Relevant factors," Sassòli said,

> ... include: intensity; number of active participants; number of victims; duration and protracted character of the violence; organization and discipline of the parties; capacity to respect [international humanitarian law]; collective, open, and coordinated character of the hostilities; direct involvement of governmental armed forces (vs. law enforcement agencies); and *de facto* authority by the non-state actor over potential victims.

The International Committee of the Red Cross (ICRC) which is charged under the Geneva Conventions with protecting the rights of prisoners of war, seems to agree with the criteria laid out by Professor Sassòli. The Red Cross has stated: "Most of the measures taken by states and others to prevent or suppress acts of terrorism do not amount to an armed conflict in either the practical or legal sense." In the ICRC's eyes, at least, much of the US war on terror is not really a war. In many cases, the kidnapping, torture, and outright murder involved have not occurred during the sort of direct clash of organized armies that most people—and most laws—define as "war."

So is the US "global war on terror" a war or not? Is it perhaps merely a metaphorical one, like a war on poverty or cancer? Or is it a genuine, sustained, armed conflict? While there is disagreement on this point, one thing is clear: The US government cannot, like Humpty Dumpty in *Alice Through the Looking Glass*, make the war on terror into a war simply by calling it one. Yet the George W. Bush administration did precisely that when in February 2002, President Bush issued a memorandum purporting to define the contours of the battle. Bush argued that

> the war against terrorism ushers in a new paradigm, one in which groups with broad, international reach commit horrific acts against innocent civilians, sometimes with the direct support of states. Our nation recognizes that this new paradigm—ushered in not by us, but by terrorists—requires new thinking in the law of war, but thinking that should nevertheless be consistent with the principles of Geneva.

In other words, in order to avoid having to treat detainees as required by the Geneva Conventions, Bush declared that his war against terrorism represented a "new paradigm," one not covered under Geneva. Nevertheless, he stated, the United States in its great magnanimity would adhere to the Geneva principles when convenient. Should these conventions prove inconvenient, Bush went on to say, "I have the authority under the Constitution to suspend Geneva as between the United States and Afghanistan, but I decline to exercise that authority at this time."

In other words, the president appeared to suggest that Geneva *does* apply, but arrogated to himself the right to unilaterally suspend an international treaty that the United States has signed and ratified! Despite whatever Bush believed, the US Constitution makes very clear that presidents may not simply suspend treaties they find bothersome. As Article VI clearly states, "This Constitution, and the laws of the United States which shall be made in pursuance thereof; *and all treaties made, or which shall be made, under the authority of the United States* [emphasis added], shall be the supreme law of the land."

As late as July 2007, Bush still maintained his ambivalent relationship with the Geneva Conventions, arguing that the war on terror was indeed a war, but that Geneva didn't apply to US detainees imprisoned in that war. In Executive Order 13440, he stated, "The United States is engaged in an armed conflict with al Qaeda, the Taliban, and associated forces," meaning that because the conflict with al Qaeda was indeed a war, the Geneva Conventions did apply. This was not problematic for the administration, however, because Bush then reiterated his decree from 2002 that neither members of the Taliban, al Qaeda, nor anyone else detained in the course of this "war" qualified as a legitimate combatant under Geneva, and that therefore their rights were more limited than those of prisoners of war. Was the president right? We'll look at this question more fully in a moment.

Apart from US operations in Afghanistan and Iraq then, I believe that the war on terror is not a war at all. It is rather the extended, apparently endless, pursuit of al Qaeda combatants in dozens of countries. Nor is al Qaeda the only enemy being pursued. As then-Defense Secretary Rumsfeld pointed out early in the war on terror, "They are just one of many networks." George W. Bush opined that the war would "not end until every terrorist group of global reach has been found, stopped and defeated." The Bush administration envisioned a war that would last for decades, if not forever. The emergence of the Islamic State in the broken countries of Iraq and Syria has only added new fuel to this endless "war."

At the start of President Obama's first term, his staff quietly replaced the expression "war on terror" with the less evocative term "overseas contingency operations." As recently as 2013, Obama told an audience at the National Defense University, "This war, like all wars, must end. That's what history advises. That's what our democracy demands." In the same speech he indicated that he intended to ask Congress to repeal the 2001 Authorization for the Use of Military Force, or AUMF, which provided a legal basis for the US invasion of Afghanistan.

All that changed, however, with the rise of the Islamic State. Far from looking for a repeal of the original AUMF, by the end of 2014 Secretary of State John Kerry was asking the Senate Foreign Relations Committee for a new authorization with the following:

1. The ability to use force against IS and associated forces,
2. No geographic limitations,
3. The option to deploy ground combat troops if necessary, and
4. An initial three-year authorization, with the option to extend.

To date, Congress has declined either to rescind the original AUMF or to pass a new one along the lines requested by

Kerry. Despite Obama's declaration that he does not "support the idea of endless war," his sprawling military and security operations have dragged on throughout his presidency. In October 2015, he announced yet another extension of the war in Afghanistan, vowing to keep US troops in that war zone through 2016, in response to a resurgence of Taliban assaults. Meanwhile, Obama expanded the air war against ISIS positions in Iraq and Syria and ordered military advisors into that growing conflict.

If the "war on terror" is not really a war, are US kidnappings, incarcerations without trial, torture, and murder then legal under international law? Do US officials have the right to do anything they want to people they perceive as enemies? Not at all. It just means that a different set of laws applies.

There are two different kinds of international law that affect how governments may treat human beings they have in their control. The Geneva Conventions, which are discussed more fully below, are part of a body of law traditionally known as International *Humanitarian* Law, or IHL. These laws cover the rights and responsibilities of all people, from state actors to private individuals, who are caught up in either an international or a non-international armed conflict. (Non-international armed conflicts are those in which the belligerents are not all state actors, as in civil wars or colonial wars of independence.) The other relevant branch of international law is International *Human Rights* Law, a set of treaties, declarations, and customs governing how states may treat people under conditions that do not amount to a full-blown "armed conflict."

I have said that I believe the US wars in Afghanistan and Iraq are indeed "international armed conflicts" in the sense intended by the Geneva Conventions. This means, as we shall see below, that anyone captured by US agents in those countries falls—in one way or another—under the protections of the Geneva Conventions and other parts of International *Humanitarian* Law. Crimes against these detainees are war crimes. On the other hand, the terrible things done to prisoners like Majid Khan, who was detained in Pakistan—an allied nation and not a war zone in the sense of Afghanistan and Iraq—are still high crimes, but they are violations of International *Human Rights* (rather than Humanitarian) Law.

The term "war crimes" has a unique rhetorical power. Its historical echoes remind us of the weight and gravity of the Nazi crimes that were prosecuted in Nuremberg. It is a shame that when the same actions—torture, disappearance, murder—happen outside the context of war, the phrase "human rights violations" that describes them does not carry the same rhetorical force. Both the crimes and the penalties may be equivalent, but somehow "crimes" sound worse than mere "violations" to the average English speaker. This is why, when it comes to considering offenses committed by officials and agents of the United States in the war on terror, I will introduce the term "crimes against human rights" to refer to the terrible abuses that take place outside the context of a traditional armed conflict.

What follows is an attempt to sort out the international and US laws that are most important in identifying US crimes and criminals of the "war on terror." If this tangle of treaties, conventions, and laws seems a bit complicated, that's because it is. Although the laws are complex, the basic number of specific crimes is relatively small, including such things as torture, enforced disappearance, illegal detention, and extrajudicial killings.

International Humanitarian Law: The Laws and Customs of War

When the Allies hammered out the London Agreement governing the Nuremberg tribunal in 1945, they defined war crimes as "violations of the laws or customs of war." What are these "laws and customs of war"? Are they still in force seventy years after Nuremberg? What relevant laws and treaties have further defined the laws and customs of war since Nuremberg?

There are quite a few laws, treaties, and customs governing how the United States and its officials are supposed to behave during wars. These agreements often raise as many questions as they resolve. For example, what *kind* of war is being waged? Is it an international conflict, that is, a war between two or more sovereign nations? If so, certain rules apply. If not, similar but separate rules come into play. Then there is the question of the *status* of an individual who has been detained during a war. Is the person being held a combatant or civilian? Different rules govern how each group should be treated. And if the person is a combatant, is he or she *legitimate* or not? Again, different rules for different people. What are the legal effects of the *declarations* and/or *reservations* that a country lists when ratifying a treaty? In the United States, does a ratified treaty have the force of federal law? If so, how can officials who violate treaties be held accountable in US courts? Consider, for example, the fact that US federal law only defines "torture" as a federal crime when it is committed *outside* the United States. How can people who have ordered or committed torture in territory under US jurisdiction, as at Guantánamo, be tried for this crime?

The idea that properly conducted wars have rules is not a new one. European views on what constitutes a "just war" go back at least to the Roman empire (much further, in fact than prohibitions on torture, which reflect relatively modern sensibilities). Most proponents of modern "just war" theory speak of three aspects of justice in war: *jus ad bellum, jus in bello,* and *jus post bellum* (justice in considering and initiating war, in the actual conduct of war, and after war has ended).*

What concerns us most at the moment are violations of the *jus in bello,* the rules governing how war should be conducted. These cover important issues such as distinguishing between combatants and non-combatants, humane treatment of captured combatants, and the prohibition of weapons that are *mala in se,* evil in and of themselves. This last includes weapons that cannot be fully controlled (or have particularly insidious effects on the human body), such as poison gas, land mines, or cluster bombs.

The 1864 and 1906 Geneva Conventions: One June day in 1859, a Swiss businessman named Henry Dunant found himself in the Italian town of Castiglione. Earlier that day in a the nearby village of Solferino, a terrible battle between French and Sardinians on one side and Austrians on the other had left nine thousand soldiers wounded, with no one caring for them. The wounded combatants had been brought to the main church in Castiglione, where the

---

* It can certainly be argued that in declaring a war involving as Donald Rumsfeld said in 2001 enemies in "50 or 60 countries" the United States may have violated one of the first rules of *jus ad bellum* – proportionality. Is a decades-long multi-continental war involving the deaths of hundreds of thousands a proportional response to the hideous "but limited" acts of terrorism committed on September 11, 2001?

horrified Dunant spent the next five days caring for them. His book describing the experience, *A Memory of Solferino,* helped launch the movement that led to the creation of the first Geneva Convention which guaranteed protection for sick and wounded soldiers and established the International Committee of the Red Cross.

In 1906, a second Geneva Convention extended these protections to naval combatants injured at sea or in shipwrecks. These conventions codified much of Europe's developing tradition of common law about warfare. The 1907 Hague Convention Respecting the Laws and Customs of War on Land extended this work, for the first time establishing rules for the treatment of prisoners: "They must be humanely treated. All their personal belongings, except arms, horses, and military papers, remain their property."

The **1949 Geneva Conventions**: The first two Geneva Conventions and the Hague Convention in turn formed the basis for the most widely invoked treaty on the conduct of war in today's world, the 1949 Geneva Conventions. Taken together, the four conventions and a fifth section, called Common Article III, make up a single treaty governing how the signatory nations will conduct themselves during wars. The four main conventions refer to *international* wars, which are wars between two or more sovereign nations. Convention One protects sick or wounded soldiers in land wars from summary execution and torture, and guarantees a right to medical attention. Convention Two extends the same protections to combatants who are either at sea or shipwrecked. Convention Three defines prisoners of war and establishes a wide variety of rights for them. Among these are the rights to recreation, to have access to a camp "commissary" (store), and to be paid a fair wage for work—rights that George W. Bush's

Attorney General Alberto Gonzales famously declared had been rendered "quaint" in the new situation created by the war on terror. Convention Four grants the same protections to civilians that apply to wounded soldiers in Convention One.

Finally, the brief but comprehensive Common Article 3 extends some of the protections in the four conventions to everyone involved in "the case of armed conflict not of an international character"—in other words, in cases of civil or other armed conflict internal to a state. Specifically, it prohibits "violence to life and person, in particular murder of all kinds, mutilation, cruel treatment and torture . . . and outrages upon personal dignity, in particular humiliating and degrading treatment."

Common Article 3 may be relevant here because some theaters of the war on terror, to the extent that it is a war at all, are "not of an international character," in the sense that they do not represent conflicts between nations. Some of the enemies defined by the United States are not nations at all, but transnational groups like al Qaeda. More important, Common Article 3 matters because, since passage of the 1996 Military Commissions Act, US law has required that detainees in the war on terror be accorded the same protections they would receive under Common Article 3—even though the Bush administration continued to maintain they were not entitled to them.

Including the United States, 196 nations have signed and ratified the Geneva Conventions. But the United States has refused to sign two additional Geneva protocols that were proposed in 1977 and ratified by 174 nations. Protocol I extends the definition of international armed conflict to "include armed conflicts in which peoples are fighting against colonial domination and alien occupation and against racist regimes." Protocol II clarifies and extends legal protections for civilian medical workers in armed conflicts.

The Role of the ICRC: The Geneva Conventions established an official role for the ICRC and its sister organizations, the Red Crescent, the Red Star, and the Sun Societies. Under the Third Geneva Convention, these organizations have the right to unrestricted access to prisoners of war in order to register and keep track of them, to verify their humane treatment, and to assist them in communications with friends and family. The ICRC may *request* access to detainees who are held in the situation covered by Common Article 3—non-international armed conflicts—but states are not required to grant it.

Prisoners of War: Under Geneva Three, prisoners of war in an international conflict have specific and extensive rights. Should the people the US has detained in its war on terror be classified as prisoners of war under Geneva Three? It depends. To qualify as a prisoner of war, a detainee must fulfill certain requirements. Article 4 of Geneva Three defines prisoners of war as people "who have fallen into the power of the enemy" (in this case, the United States) and are also combatants, such as

> 1) Members of the armed forces of a Party to the conflict as well as members of militias or volunteer corps forming part of such armed forces.

or:

> 2) Members of other militias and members of other volunteer corps, including those of organized resistance movements, belonging to a Party to the conflict and operating in or outside their own territory, even if

this territory is occupied, provided that such militias or volunteer corps, including such organized resistance movements, fulfill the following conditions:

    a) that of being commanded by a person responsible for his subordinates;

    b) that of having a fixed distinctive sign recognizable at a distance;

    c) that of carrying arms openly;

    d) that of conducting their operations in accordance with the laws and customs of war.

Various noncombatants, including civilians like journalists and medical staff, who are traveling with an army or militia are also covered.

In February 2002 President Bush issued a memorandum declaring that none of the people detained by the United States in Afghanistan—neither Taliban nor al Qaeda—counted as prisoners of war. He argued that the Taliban did not wear uniforms or some other "fixed sign" that made them recognizable. Therefore, they did not qualify as combatants under Geneva Three. However, as Kenneth Roth, head of Human Rights Watch, pointed out in the *New York Times*, the Taliban were in fact the government of Afghanistan when the United States invaded, and therefore their fighters were members of that country's armed forces. In other words, the members of the Taliban captured in Afghanistan are entitled to all the protections under Geneva Three. This includes, under Article 17, the right not to be tortured or in any way punished for refusing to answer questions in interrogations.

No physical or mental torture, nor any other form of coercion [emphasis added], may be inflicted on prisoners of war to secure from them information of any kind whatever. Prisoners of war who refuse to answer may not be threatened, insulted, or exposed to unpleasant or disadvantageous treatment of any kind.

That seems pretty clear.

But what about members of al Qaeda captured in Afghanistan? Aren't they, as the Bush administration argued, unlawful combatants, and therefore not covered under Geneva Three? In fact, the Geneva conventions make no mention of the term "unlawful" combatants. It does seem that al Qaeda members picked up in Afghanistan (or those suspected of being members of al Qaeda) were not combatants in the US–Afghanistan war as defined by international law. They were not a militia serving the Afghan government, nor part of a clearly defined chain of command, nor did they wear a "fixed distinctive sign recognizable at a distance." So, if they were not combatants, were they covered under the Geneva Conventions at all—or did they simply fall outside the legal protections of the laws and customs of war?

Odd as it may seem, many experts believe that if non-Taliban individuals picked up in Afghanistan were not combatants, then they were civilians. The ICRC understands the four Geneva Conventions as a seamless whole; no one who is caught up in an international armed conflict is left outside the convention's protection. This is spelled out in the commentary section of Geneva Four:

Every person in enemy hands must have some status under international law: he is either a prisoner of war and, as such, covered by the Third Convention, a civilian covered by the Fourth Convention, or again, a member of the medical personnel of the armed forces who is covered by the First Convention. There is no intermediate status; nobody in enemy hands can be outside the law.

People who are protected under Geneva Four also have the right to visits by the Red Cross. If the power holding these detainees fails to register them, hides them or treats them as "ghost prisoners"—as the CIA has treated many detainees—this is a violation of the Fourth Geneva Convention.

Once captured, members of al Qaeda taken in Afghanistan would seem to also be covered under Article 3 of Geneva Three, which protects anyone who is not actively involved in an international armed conflict, including people who cannot fight any longer because they have been detained. Such people, simply because of their presence in a country at war, also have some rights, although not the same ones given to prisoners of war. They must be treated humanely and protected from "violence to life and person, in particular murder of all kinds, mutilation, cruel treatment and torture." Nor may the nation holding them expose them to "outrages upon personal dignity, in particular, humiliating and degrading treatment." In other words, pretty much everything that the United States did to its Taliban as well as non-Taliban prisoners was illegal, from the time they were picked up in Afghanistan, until—by whatever circuitous route—they found themselves incarcerated in the US prison camp at Guantánamo Bay or rendered to some other country.

What about people whom the CIA or other US forces have snatched up in other places around the world—people like Khalid El-Masri, who was abducted while on holiday in

Macedonia?* What about people "arrested" in Italy, Pakistan, or the Philippines? Are they prisoners of war under Geneva Three? The short answer is no, because they weren't seized in a country where an international armed conflict (a war between two or more nations) is taking place. In that case, are they covered by Common Article 3, which protects people captured in a *non*-international armed conflict? Probably not, because, apart from the military conflicts in Afghanistan and Iraq, the war on terror isn't really a war at all in the legal sense. There is another entire body of law, however, that covers these atrocities, which we'll examine after we see what US domestic laws of war exist.

US Laws of War

The moment the United States ratified the Geneva Accords, they became, like any ratified treaty, the "supreme law of the land" under Article VI of the US Constitution. There are also some purely domestic laws governing US conduct in war. The ones that are relevant here are relatively recent. Let's take a look at them.

The 1996 War Crimes Act: Also identified as US Code §2441, the War Crimes Act establishes penalties for members of the US armed forces and any US national who commits a war crime. In particular, any "grave breach" of the

---

* El-Masri's case is particularly egregious. In 2003, the Macedonian police handed him over to the CIA, which shipped him to the notorious "Salt Pit" (CIA black site "COBALT" in the Senate Select Intelligence Committee's report on CIA torture). There he was beaten and raped, and had a gun held to his head. After four months he was dumped on a rural road in Albania. It seems the CIA had arrested the wrong man. The wanted some *other* Khalid el-Masri, not, as Amy Davidson wrote in the *New Yorker*, the "car salesman from Bavaria."

1949 Geneva Conventions, including Common Article 3, constitutes a war crime. More explicitly, the War Crimes Act criminalizes torture, cruel or inhuman treatment, performing biological experiments, murder, mutilation or maiming, intentionally causing serious bodily harm, rape, and sexual assault or abuse. Each of these offenses is further described (and circumscribed) with reference to other parts of the US legal code, including § 2340, which defines the crime of torture, and which we'll be examining more carefully later on.

The Detainee Treatment Act: Congress passed this piece of US law in 2006, as an amendment to that year's Defense Appropriations Act. It requires that all detainees in US custody be treated according to the rules in the *US Army Field Manual on Intelligence Interrogation*. At the time the field manual prohibited most of the torture that the CIA and other intelligence agencies had used on detainees. However, a classified section, Appendix M, still permitted solitary confinement for up to thirty days, sleep deprivation (with a required four hours of sleep every twenty-four hours) and up to twelve hours of sensory deprivation. In the newest version, called the *US Army Field Manual on Human Intelligence Collector Operations*, Appendix M has been declassified. The UN Committee Against Torture flagged this appendix—among many other concerns—in its 2014 report on US compliance with the Convention against Torture and Other Cruel, Inhuman, or Degrading Treatment or Punishment (CAT).

The Detainee Treatment Act also contained a provision designed to protect from prosecution any agent of the US government who did *anything* to a detainee (including treatment prohibited in the *Army Field Manual*) as long as the person "did not know that the practices were unlawful and a person of ordinary sense and understanding would not know the practices were unlawful." How were torturers and their superiors supposed to know whether what they were doing was unlawful? The law provides an answer. "Good faith reliance on advice of counsel should be an important factor, among others, to consider in assessing whether a person of ordinary sense and understanding would have known the practices to be unlawful."

In other words, the Detainee Treatment Act attempted to shield torturers from prosecution (and gave the government permission to pay for their legal defense), so long as they had followed the advice of government lawyers like John Yoo and Jay Bybee. The infamous 2002 memo written by Yoo and Bybee stated that "in order to constitute torture" and hence to violate US law, a victim's pain must be so great that it would "ordinarily be associated with a sufficiently serious physical condition or injury such as death, organ failure, or serious impairment of bodily functions . . . ." In other words, if the victim didn't actually die, he wasn't tortured. Any "person of ordinary sense and understanding" knows that.

Another section of the Detainee Treatment Act also explicitly denied the right of *habeas corpus* to any prisoner being held by the Department of Defense at Guantánamo. The Supreme Court overturned this section in its decision in *Hamdan v. Rumsfeld,* ruling that the Guantánamo detainees had the right under Geneva Common Article 3 to be tried in a "a regularly constituted court." The "military commissions" the Bush administration had set up did not qualify because they did not operate under the Uniform Code of Military Justice. (We revisit the *Hamdan* decision in Chapter 4.)

However, Justice Stephen Breyer pointed out that although these commissions were illegal, "nothing prevents the President from returning to Congress to seek the authority he believes necessary" to create tribunals that would satisfy the requirements of Common Article 3— which is exactly what the Bush administration did. The result was the Military Commissions Act of 2006, which established "commissions" to try those being detained at Guantánamo. Once again, the administration sought to deny the right of *habeas corpus* to detainees, on the ground that they had now established "a regularly constituted court," and once again, the Supreme Court disagreed. In its 2008 *Boumediene v. Bush* ruling, the court concluded that Lakhdar Boumediene, a citizen of Bosnia and Herzegovina, did in fact have the right to challenge his detention under *habeas corpus.*

In short, then, US and international humanitarian laws define the rights and protections that people should have when they are caught up, voluntarily or otherwise, in a war. And even though the US government, particularly the Bush administration, has repeatedly tried to reinterpret these international and domestic laws to suit its own purposes, courts have resisted this effort.

What about people detained in a conflict that is not a traditional war? Are there legal remedies for those who are tortured, disappeared, or killed in conflicts that don't qualify as wars? Yes, there are. Such people fall under the protection of domestic US criminal laws as well as international human rights law (IHRL).

International Human Rights Law

The United States has signed a number of international treaties that make up the body of IHRL, including the 1976 International Covenant on Civil and Political Rights (ICCPR) and the 1984 Convention against Torture and Other Cruel, Inhuman, or Degrading Treatment or Punishment (CAT). Both of these will be discussed below.

There are also several treaties, promulgated either by the United Nations or the Organization of American States, that many human rights experts wish the United States had signed, but which it has not. These include the Inter-American Convention to Prevent and Punish Torture; the American Convention on Human Rights (which the United States signed but never ratified); and the United Nations International Convention for the Protection of All Persons from Enforced Disappearance.

Perhaps the most important IHRL treaty the United States has failed to ratify is the one establishing the International Criminal Court, a court of last resort for trying cases of war crimes and crimes against humanity. Under President Bill Clinton in 2000, the United States signed the Rome Statute, which established the court. But in 2002, President Bush notified the United Nations that the United States was rescinding its signature and had no intention to ratify the accord. That same year Congress passed the American Servicemembers Protection Act, which explicitly outlaws US cooperation with the ICC. The Obama administration's attitude toward the ICC has been more conciliatory, but no actual movement towards ratification has taken place.

1976 International Covenant on Civil and Political Rights (ICCPR): The United States did ratify the ICCPR in 1992, after a delay of almost two decades. This covenant contains some important measures that, like any other ratified treaty, should be considered part of US federal law. These include Article 7, which states, "No one shall be subjected to torture or to cruel, inhuman or degrading treatment or punishment."

The ICCPR does not explicitly prohibit enforced disappearance. It does, however, hold that "[n]o one shall be subjected to arbitrary arrest or detention." Furthermore, "[e]veryone shall have the right to recognition everywhere as a person before the law." This is a right that cannot be enforced when someone is being held incommunicado, without access to friends, family, legal counsel or international aid groups like the Red Cross.

1984 United Nations Convention against Torture and Other Cruel, Inhuman, or Degrading Treatment or Punishment (CAT): The UN CAT is the most important international treaty on torture. The United States ratified it in 1984, and it remains federal law. Here is how the UN convention defines torture. It is

> *any act by which severe pain or suffering, whether physical or mental, is intentionally inflicted on a person* for such purposes as obtaining from him or a third person information or a confession, punishing him for an act he or a third person has committed or is suspected of having committed, or intimidating or coercing him or a third person, or for any reason based on discrimination of any kind, *when such pain or suffering is inflicted by or at the instigation of or with the consent or acquiescence of a public official or other person acting in an official capacity* [emphasis added].

Not only does the CAT prohibit torture by any person acting in an official capacity, it outlaws another practice that has been common in the US war on terror: extraordinary rendition. In other words, no signatory to the convention may do what the United States did to many unfortunate people who were swept up in its international dragnet after 9/11.

Among these was Binyam Mohammed, who was detained in Pakistan, tortured there, and then sent at US request to Morocco. There, at least once a month for eighteen months, Moroccan guards sliced his penis open with a scalpel, making twenty to thirty cuts over the course of a couple of hours.* What happened to Mohammed (and hundreds of others) is against the law under the CAT. Article 3 states explicitly that "no State Party shall expel, return . . . or extradite a person to another State where there are substantial grounds for believing that he would be in danger of being subjected to torture."

Is the United States still involved in extraordinary renditions? We don't know for sure. The day after he took office in 2009, President Obama signed an executive order that banned the use of torture in interrogations and ordered the CIA "black sites" closed. The order did not, however, prohibit rendition. Rather, it referred the matter to a Special Interagency Task Force on Interrogation and Transfer Policies. The task force submitted its recommendations to the president in August 2009. On the question of rendition, it said, "When the United States transfers individuals to other countries, it may rely on assurances from the receiving country" that the individuals will not be tortured." This seems to be very weak protection indeed. What country is going to put in writing its intention to torture someone?

---

* The apparent purpose of this torment was to get Mohammed to implicate U.S. citizen José Padilla in a plot to explode a "dirty bomb" somewhere in the United States. Under torture, Mohammed finally broke down and told his captors what they wanted to hear, although he has since recanted. When the United States finally prosecuted and convicted Padilla in a civilian court, the charges made no mention of the dirty bomb plot, which it now seems likely was a CIA invention created and corroborated through torture.

The framers of the UN Convention against Torture knew that governments that resort to torture look for justifications for their practices. That is why Article 2 stated so clearly that "*no exceptional circumstances whatsoever* [emphasis added],whether a state of war or a threat of war, internal political instability or any other public emergency, may be invoked as a justification of torture."

During the 2008 presidential campaign, Obama was critical of the worst excesses of the Bush administration's war on terror, but after his election, he made it clear that prosecutions of Bush officials were off the table. In January 2009, Obama announced that he was not going to authorize a serious inquiry into the crimes of the past, famously stating, "We need to look forward as opposed to looking backwards."

Years later in 2014, Obama admitted that "we tortured some folks." He was speaking days before the release of the 500-page executive summary of the investigation conducted by the Senate Select Committee on Intelligence into the CIA torture program. "We tortured some folks." It was a strangely mild way to describe the rampant human rights abuses and war crimes committed during the war on terror. Obama tried further to take the sting out of the Senate committee's imminent torture report by advising those who read it "not to feel too sanctimonious in retrospect about the tough job those [CIA] folks had," adding, "A lot of those folks were working hard under enormous pressure and are real patriots."

The widespread public fear in America following the 9/11 attacks, Obama seemed to say, justified the government's brutal response. The public officials who instigated and acquiesced to torture had a good reason: they were scared. "It is important, when we look back," said the president, "to recall how afraid people were after the twin towers fell, and the Pentagon had been hit, and the plane in Pennsylvania had fallen and people did not know whether more attacks were imminent."

The president was, of course, simply wrong. Torturers are not immune from legal judgment because their jobs are "tough," nor does public fear grant a government the authority to violate international human rights laws. The Convention against Torture *requires* the United States to establish criminal penalties for torture and to bring prosecutions against all those responsible. The failure to do so is itself a violation of international human rights law.

US Human Rights Law

The United States has a fairly large body of human rights law, beginning with the first ten amendments to the Constitution, known as the Bill of Rights. It is the Bill of Rights that encodes, among other rights, Americans' freedom of the press and of religion, our right to trial by jury and exemption from self-incrimination, our protections against cruel and unusual punishment, and our right to assemble "peaceably" to demand redress of our grievances from the government. When the Senate finally ratified the UN Convention against Torture, it added to the body of law protecting individuals from the abuses of authorities. But US Code §2340, the implementing legislation for the Convention against Torture passed in 1994, defined torture a bit more narrowly than the CAT did. Code §2340 prohibits the brutal practice—but *only when it takes place outside territory controlled by the United States.* Successive administrations have argued that there is no need to create a separate federal crime for torture inside the United States because both federal and state laws already prohibit assault, battery, murder, kidnapping, and so forth.

Only one person has ever been convicted of a crime under §2340. He is Charles McArther Emmanuel, otherwise known as Chuckie Taylor or Roy Belfast, Jr.—a son of Charles Taylor, the former Liberian dictator. Emmanuel, a US citizen, was convicted of torture for activities during the Liberian civil war and sentenced to ninety-seven years in prison.

Apart from torture committed in Guantánamo, which is under US jurisdiction even though it's located in Cuba, the torture of detainees in any other part of the world is prohibited under the Geneva Conventions, the CAT, the ICCPR, and numerous US laws, including US Code §2340.

The Nuremberg Principles

The United Nations General Assembly adopted the Nuremberg Principles in 1950, but their status as international law is much debated. The nations signing the UN charter intentionally chose not to grant the UN the power to create law through legislation. To this day, the two extant forms of international law remain the unwritten "laws and customs" of nations and the written treaties and conventions subscribed to by individual countries. Where do the Nuremberg Principles fit? Certainly the International Law Commission, which produced the principles at the request of the General Assembly, intended them to form part of the corpus of international law. In fact, the principles have guided war crimes prosecutions in Yugoslavia and Rwanda. It is fair to say that they articulate concepts that have become deeply incorporated in the laws and customs of war.

At least one of the innovative concepts incorporated in the Nuremberg Principles has special relevance for the consideration of war crimes during the war on terror. The principles specifically prohibited the "waging of a war of

The following table illustrates the various laws under which US officials and private contractors can and should be held accountable for their crimes:

Year	Type of Law		Relevant Crimes
	Humanitarian Law		
	International Law	**US Federal Law**	
1907	Hague Conventions		• Mistreatment of prisoners • Pillage • Failure to care for sick or injured
1949	Geneva Conventions		• Torture • Forced disappearance • Murder • Rape and sexual assault • War crimes
1950	Nuremberg Principles		• Planning and making aggressive war • War crimes • Crimes against humanity, including persecution based on religion or race

Year	Type of Law		Relevant Crimes
	Humanitarian Law		
	International Law	**US Federal Law**	
1996		War Crimes Act (US Code 18 § 2441)	• Grave breaches of the Geneva Conventions • Torture • Cruel, inhuman, or degrading treatment • Mutilation or maiming • Rape • Sexual assault or abuse
2005		Detainee Treatment Act	• Interrogation techniques not included in *US Army Field Manual on Human Intelligence Collector Operations*
	Human Rights Law		
	International Law	**US Federal Law**	
1976	International Covenant on Civil and Political Rights		• Torture • Cruel, inhuman, or degrading treatment • Enforced disappearance

Year	Type of Law	Relevant Crimes
1984	U.N Convention against Torture and Other Cruel, Inhuman, or Degrading Treatment or Punishment	• Torture • Cruel, inhuman, or degrading treatment
1994	US Code §2340	• Torture committed outside the United States

Chapter 3

Crimes Against Peace

———————

Then another horse came out, a fiery red one. Its rider was given power to take peace from the earth and to make people kill each other. To him was given a large sword.

—Revelation 6:4, The Holy Bible
(New International Version)

To initiate a war of aggression is not only an international crime; it is the supreme international crime, differing only from other war crimes in that it contains within itself the accumulated evil of the whole.

—Judgment of the International
Military Tribunal at Nuremberg

When I told a friend that one of the crimes I'd be considering in *American Nuremberg* is "waging an aggressive war," she was startled. "But isn't every war an aggressive war?" she asked. "That's like saying waging war is illegal in itself." In a way my friend was right. In most cases, starting a war *is* illegal under the laws and customs of war, especially because starting a war usually involves one country's invasion of another's territory. The Americans fought to establish the primacy of crimes against peace in the planning stages for Nuremberg. The other Nazi crimes, they argued, sprang from the original crime of planning and then in 1939 launching an unprovoked war. No war, no war crimes.

Is there a similar "original crime" from which the crimes of the US war on terror spring? I believe there is. It is the planning and execution of the unprovoked war that the United States launched against Iraq in 2003. Within a few hours of the al Qaeda attacks on 9/11, Defense Secretary Donald Rumsfeld and his deputy Paul Wolfowitz were already arguing that this was the justification the Bush administration had been waiting for to attack Iraq. "Dealing with Iraq would show a major commitment to antiterrorism," Rumsfeld insisted, as George W. Bush later recalled in his memoir. Of course, as the world later learned, there was no evidence that Saddam Hussein's regime was behind the terror attacks on New York and Washington—and there never would be such evidence. As we shall see, however, the planning for "dealing with Iraq" had been underway for years.

Even during the run-up to the Iraq War, the Bush administration committed human rights crimes as it tried to build a case for war, authorizing the torture of people to produce evidence that Saddam was behind 9/11. In 2002, the CIA shipped a Libyan named Ibn al-Shaykh al-Libi, who probably had been an al Qaeda trainer, to Egypt. There he was waterboarded until he agreed to the proposition that, as President Bush put it in an October 2002 speech to the nation, "Iraq has trained al Qaeda in bomb-making and poisons and deadly gases." In the same speech, Bush even explained where this "information" had come from, saying, "Evidence from intelligence sources, secret communications *and statements by people now in custody* [emphasis added] reveal that Saddam Hussein aids and protects terrorists, including members of al Qaeda." Then-Secretary of State Colin Powell repeated this claim in his now infamous speech to the UN Security Council justifying US military action against Iraq. al-Libi later recanted, saying his statement implicating Iraq had been forced out of him under torture, but by then the war was well underway.

The CIA was not the only agency that tortured people to develop "intelligence" on a hoped-for Iraq–al Qaeda connection. This also seems to have been the main reason that the Defense Department first introduced torture at Guantánamo. In 2008, the Senate Armed Services Committee held hearings on the military's treatment of the people it had detained in the war on terror, producing a report entitled "Inquiry into the Treatment of Detainees in US Custody." The Senate committee wanted to understand how the rules for interrogations at Guantánamo had been established. By that time, it was well known that Donald Rumsfeld had approved a memo prepared by his chief counsel, William "Jim" Haynes, outlining permitted interrogation techniques. These techniques included several that amount to torture: threatening detainees or their families with injury or death, isolation, exposure to cold "weather or water," use of painful stress positions, sensory deprivation, enforced nudity, and exploitation of phobias, among others.

The Senate Armed Services Committee investigation helped explain why, starting in November 2002, there was increasing pressure from Rumsfeld's office on down the ranks for more extreme methods of interrogation. In 2006, the Army Inspector General interviewed a Major Paul Burney, who had been stationed at Guantánamo at the time. "[A] large part of the time we were focused on trying to establish a link between al Qaeda and Iraq," he told the IG, "and we were not being successful in establishing a link between al Qaeda and Iraq. The more frustrated people got in not being able to establish that link, there was more and more pressure to resort to measures that might produce more immediate results." David Becker, chief of Guantánamo's Interrogation Control Element (ICE), testified that he too came under substantial pressure, including from the office of Deputy Defense Secretary Wolfowitz, to "use more aggressive tactics." Wolfowitz, as we shall see, was a key player in rushing the United States to war with Iraq.

Of all the crimes connected to the endless "war" on terror, starting this genuine war with Iraq might well have been the worst. There is a reason why crimes against peace are considered *crimes*. Two thousand years ago, the writers of the biblical Book of Revelation seated War on one of the four horses that signal the world's end. The coming of War signaled complete desolation and was followed inevitably by the rider of the pale horse, Death. Since those ancient days, war's cruelty has only expanded with the growth of the vast technology of violence.

For people in the United States, where no war has been fought on domestic soil since the 1860s, it is difficult to understand what it means to live in a country at war. US veterans and their friends and families, of course, have more of an idea, but even the military's experience of war is qualitatively different from what civilians go through. Like World War II, the Iraq War has killed many more civilians than fighters. War disrupts every part of ordinary life, even when the battlefields are far away. It can divide families, and sunder relations within and between neighborhoods, communities, and religious and ethnic groups. It can destroy an entire generation of economic and educational progress. In an agrarian society, war disrupts the cycle of planting and harvest, sometimes for years. Famine, disease, and suffering without relief, will often follow. Modern war also creates environmental havoc, leaving land unusable for decades, studded with land mines or unexploded cluster bombs, or permeated with toxic chemicals like dioxin or undepleted uranium. Along with this poisoning of the environment often come medical calamities, as evidenced in Iraq, which is now suffering sharp spikes in cancers, respiratory diseases and birth defects.

It is precisely because war engenders such devastation that the international community today usually considers initiating a war to be a criminal undertaking.

If it is difficult for those who have not experienced war to imagine its horror on a personal level, it is perhaps even harder for the human mind to encompass the suffering of millions. Oxford evolutionary psychologist Robin Dunbar suggests that most people's social circle numbers between 150 and 200 individuals. These are the people who are most real to us, the ones we "know." Beyond that number, people fade into abstraction. Perhaps we can extrapolate from larger aggregations we've experienced. I know what 70,000 people feels like, because I sat with that many once in a Soweto stadium, celebrating South African Youth Day and listening to Nelson Mandela speak and Miriam Makeba sing. The crowd was so big, my feet left the ground as I was swept into the arena. Can I now imagine adding thirteen more stadiums with the same size crowd to that collection of humanity? Only then would I come close to imagining the immensity of a million persons, each with a story, a life.

What about the War in Afghanistan?

I have chosen not to include the initiation of the US war against Afghanistan among US crimes against peace for two reasons. First, although I personally believe that, like the war against Iraq, this war was illegal, there is much less agreement about this. Most of the world's nations, including countries that opposed the invasion of Iraq, supported the United States in going to war with Afghanistan. Second, those who began the Afghanistan war are precisely the same people who promoted the war in Iraq. Indeed, for many of them, Afghanistan was just a stop along the way to the true destination. So the omission of Afghanistan does not imply that these warmakers are being given a free pass.

The Iraq War has caused as many as a million human deaths and many more injuries; has uprooted millions more; and has left what was once a modern, developed nation of twenty-four million people in utter physical, political, and economic shambles. The invasion, accompanied by ruthless aerial attacks in Baghdad—and followed by years of abusive, poorly planned, and under-staffed occupation—unleashed an earthquake of destabilization that continues to shake the region today. In the years following the invasion, over a million refugees fled to neighboring countries like Syria and Jordan. The latter's population already included millions of

Palestinian refugees. As many as 2.5 million Iraqis became internally displaced.

And the damage continues to this day. Far from solving the problem of terrorism with "shock and awe," the Iraq War has plowed the field for a new crop of terrorist associations, now coalescing under the banner of the so-called Islamic State. Instead of bringing "stability" to Iraq and the larger region, the war brought to a boil long-simmering class, ethnic and sectarian hostilities in Iraqi society and has rendered ordinary life almost impossible for more than a decade.

The attacks of 9/11 and the declaration of a global war on terror provided a pretext for this war, but it had been planned long before. In public, the war's proponents—including officials like George W. Bush, Dick Cheney, Donald Rumsfeld, and Condoleezza Rice—argued that bringing "freedom" to Iraq would ultimately bring greater stability to the whole region. A month before the invasion, in February 2003, Bush explained this strategy to an audience at the conservative American Enterprise Institute. Getting rid of Saddam Hussein would not only protect Americans from a "direct and growing threat;" it would stabilize the entire Middle East:

> Acting against the danger will also contribute greatly to the long-term safety and stability of our world. The current Iraqi regime has shown the power of tyranny to spread discord and violence in the Middle East. A liberated Iraq can show the power of freedom to transform that vital region, by bringing hope and progress into the lives of millions. America's interests in security, and America's belief in liberty, both lead in the same direction: to a free and peaceful Iraq.

In fact, despite whatever Bush himself may have believed, the US war on Iraq was never intended to stabilize the Middle East. The real goal of those who planned and carried out the war was precisely the opposite—to shake up the existing power dynamics in the region and produce a new alignment, one that would benefit the economic and strategic interests of the United States and Israel. Nevertheless, waging war for *either* purpose—for Bush's pre-emptive self-defense or to advance US interests by changing power relations in the Middle East—is legally inexcusable. It is a crime against peace.

The international rule of law was not uppermost in their minds, however, when in 1996, Cheney's fellow war hawks Richard Perle and Douglas Feith participated in a study group that advocated just this realignment strategy. The study group's brief paper, written for the newly elected Israeli Prime Minister Benjamin Netanyahu, was called "A Clean Break: A New Strategy for Securing the Realm." The report urged the leaders of Israel's right-wing Likud Party to make a clean break with the nation's previous geopolitical strategy, to abandon Israel's peace negotiations with the Palestinians like those that led to the Oslo Accords, and instead to use military means to actively restructure the Middle East.

The authors argued that "Israel can shape its strategic environment, in cooperation with Turkey and Jordan, by weakening, containing, and even rolling back Syria." Such a campaign would begin by "removing Saddam Hussein from power in Iraq—an important Israeli strategic objective in its own right—as a means of foiling Syria's regional ambitions." The ultimate goal would be a realignment of power in the Middle East, with Syria destabilized, a Hashemite king ruling Iraq, and a new regional alliance among Turkey, Jordan, and Israel.

Today, Syria has certainly been "rolled back" in a civil war that has claimed hundreds of thousands of lives. In July 2015, the UN High Commissioner for Refugees announced that the war had displaced over half of Syria's pre-war population of twenty-two million. A third of those twelve million souls—a staggering four million people—are now refugees outside Syria, with many desperately seeking asylum in Europe and the US. The tragic images of children and entire families washing up dead on the shores of European countries are, in effect, just one more aspect of the humanitarian disaster caused by the Bush administration's invasion of Iraq. The US invasion did not cause the Syrian civil war, but it unleashed the shock waves—as Perle and his co-authors predicted and hoped—that made it possible, as well as creating the conditions for the rise of extremist forces like the Islamic State.

At the time, Netanyahu rejected the "Clean Break" paper, perhaps because one of its key suggestions was that Israel should also make a clean break from its dependence on US aid. But Richard Perle was undeterred. January 1998 found him at the head of a group of neoconservatives, many of them former advisors to Ronald Reagan, who had gathered under the name Project for a New American Century. PNAC wrote to President Bill Clinton, encouraging him to direct "a full complement of diplomatic, political and military efforts" in order to "remove Saddam Hussein from power."

Nor did the PNAC letter signers much care whether such an action would be legal under international law, although they thought it might be. "We believe the US has the authority under existing UN resolutions to take the necessary steps, including military steps, to protect our vital interests in the Gulf," they argued. But whether or not the world agreed, they continued, "American policy cannot continue to be crippled by a misguided insistence on unanimity in the UN Security

Council." In other words, while the United States should be free to use its veto power to block the wishes of other Security Council members, it should not allow itself to be "crippled" by adherence to the UN charter, whose Article 51 only permits unilateral war-making without the prior approval of the Security Council for purposes of immediate "individual or collective self-defense if an armed attack occurs against a Member of the United Nations."

The list of those who signed the PNAC letter reads like a *Who's Who* of the neoconservative elite who helped pave the intellectual path to the Iraq nightmare: Elliott Abrams, Richard L. Armitage, William J. Bennett, Jeffrey Bergner, John Bolton, Paula Dobriansky, Francis Fukuyama, Robert Kagan, Zalmay Khalilzad, William Kristol, Richard Perle, Peter W. Rodman, Donald Rumsfeld, William Schneider, Jr., Vin Weber, Paul Wolfowitz, R. James Woolsey, and Robert B. Zoellick.

Many of these people found work in the new administration of George W. Bush. For instance, Elliott Abrams (known for his role in the Iran-Contra affair under Reagan) became a special assistant to President Bush as well as a senior official at the National Security Council.

Richard Armitage served on candidate Bush's foreign policy advisors' group, led by Condoleezza Rice. After Bush became president, Armitage was made a State Department undersecretary, serving until 2005, when he was succeeded by another PNAC letter signer, Robert Zoellick.

PNAC signer John Bolton, another veteran of the Reagan-era Iran–Contra scandal, became Bush's undersecretary of State for arms control. In that capacity he torpedoed a 2001 Geneva meeting on implementation of the 1972 International Biological Weapons Convention by refusing US cooperation with a proposed enforcement regime. In other words, even as the United States was demanding weapons inspections in Iraq, Bolton made sure no such inspections would take place in this country. "As a result," observed *USA Today* in 2003—with no apparent irony—"there is no practical mechanism to stop the spread of biological weapons."

The *Los Angeles Times* credited Bolton with also engineering the 2002 dismissal of José Bustani, the head of the UN's Organization for the Prohibition of Chemical Weapons, which was involved in overseeing Iraq's disarmament process. A former Bolton deputy told the *Times* that Bolton's problem with Bustani was that the UN official "was trying to send chemical-weapons inspectors to Baghdad in advance of the US-led invasion." Presumably Bolton didn't want the UN trumpeting the bad news that Iraq had no active chemical weapons program. In 2005, Bolton became US ambassador to the United Nations, where he continued to do what he could to obstruct an institution for which he had frequently evidenced considerable contempt.

Born in Afghanistan, PNAC's Zalmay Khalilzad has a long record of US government service alternating with stints in government-connected think tanks like the RAND Corporation. Khalilzad assisted Jimmy Carter's hawkish national security advisor, Zbigniew Brzezinski, in promoting a policy to support the groups of Muslim fighters known as mujahideen (who would eventually form the nucleus of the Taliban) in their fight to oust the Soviets from Afghanistan. In Ronald Reagan's State Department, he continued the strategy of supporting the mujahideen in Afghanistan and helped shaped Reagan policy on the Iran–Iraq war.

Khalilzad played several roles in the George W. Bush administration, first heading up the Defense Department transition team and then serving as a special assistant to the President and a member of his National Security Council. Then, in

December 2002, months before the US invasion of Iraq, the White House announced Khalizad's appointment as Special Envoy and Ambassador at Large for Free Iraqis. According to the White House press release, "As Special Envoy, Dr. Khalilzad will serve as the focal point for contacts and coordination among Free Iraqis for the United States Government and *for preparations for a post-Saddam Hussein Iraq* [emphasis added]." Later he served the Bush administration as ambassador to Afghanistan, Iraq, and the United Nations.

Paul Wolfowitz, one of the signers of the "Clean Break" paper and today a visiting scholar at the American Enterprise Institute, is another policymaker with a long history of militaristic advocacy, having served both Democrats and Republicans as far back as the 1970s. When the Project for a New American Century wrote to President Clinton recommending military action to remove Saddam Hussein, the group was taking a page out of Wolfowitz's playbook. When the committee insisted that "American policy should not continue to be crippled" by the rules of the UN Security Council, it was echoing a view Wolfowitz had put forward as early as 1992. In that year, he supervised creation of a document called the "Defense Planning Guidance" while serving as undersecretary of defense for policy under Dick Cheney, who was at that time George H. W. Bush's defense secretary. The then-classified DPG, as it came to be known, fell into the hands of the *New York Times* and caused considerable consternation when its publication revealed that the first President Bush was contemplating a new world order in which the United States was prepared to take unilateral military action when it felt like it:

> The perceived capability of the US *to act independently*, if necessary, is thus an important factor even in those

cases where we do not actually do so. It will not always be incumbent upon us to assume a leadership role. In some cases, we will promote the assumption of leadership by others, such as the United Nations or regional organizations. But we will not ignore the need to be prepared to protect our critical interests and honor our commitments with only limited additional help, *or even alone*, if necessary [emphasis added].

The document carried Wolfowitz's signature, but one of its actual two authors was Zalmay Khalilizad. Long-time Dick Cheney operative Lewis "Scooter" Libby was also involved, as marginal notes on the declassified document made clear.

When George W. Bush was elected, Wolfowitz found himself at the center of power, too. Indeed, by 2001, the neocons were fully ensconced in the Bush administration, with Wolfowitz, Perle and Feith in key positions at the Pentagon, where Don Rumsfeld, another signer of the warmongering PNAC letter to Clinton, was of course installed as secretary of defense. Meanwhile, Dick Cheney—another key member of this hawkish circle—held the reins as vice president, aided by fellow hardliners like Scooter Libby. After the attacks of 9/11, these men finally were in a position to bring about the first phase of the program they'd endorsed years before. A war to unseat Saddam Hussein in Iraq would announce the United States' willingness to act unilaterally to "protect our critical interests," as they had suggested back in 1992.

Why Iraq? To begin with, there were old hostilities. For much of the cold war, Iraq had enjoyed close ties with the Soviet Union while maintaining chilly relations with Washington. These facts did not, however, prevent the United States from "tilting" towards Iraq in its eight-year war against Iran from 1980 to 1988, a human slaughterhouse that the Reagan adminstration helped fuel by supplying Iraq with weapons, money, and intelligence from US satellites. The Reagan-Bush administration threw its support behind Saddam during this bloody regional conflict as a bulwark against revolutionary Iran, which had overthrown the US-backed Shah Mohammad Reza Pahlavi and seized the US embassy in Tehran in 1979. When Saddam used mustard and nerve gas against Iranian soldiers and civilians, and later against his own people in the Kurdish region, the Reagan-Bush government simply looked the other way. From the war against Iran until the Iraqi invasion of Kuwait in 1990, Baghdad was a US ally, prized for providing a counterweight against revolutionary Iran and for the Saddam regime's secular, development-minded stance—not to mention its wealth of oil reserves.

All that changed with the first Gulf War in 1991. US forces, supported financially and logistically by Saudi Arabia, drove Iraq out of Kuwait, but left Saddam Hussein's battered regime in place. By all objective accounts, Saddam's rule was a vicious one, marked by violent repression, widespread torture, and the political and economic domination of a majority Shia country by the Sunni Muslim minority (through the largely Sunni Ba'ath party). It did not, however, present "a direct and growing threat" to the "safety of the American people." By the time the United States invaded in 2003, Iraq's economy had been all but shattered by years of war and international economic sanctions. Its stockpiles of chemical and biological weapons had been largely destroyed, and the country's remaining arsenal was old and decaying and under continual UN observation.

In early March 2003, chief UN weapons inspector Hans Blix told the Security Council that Iraq had shown "active" and even "proactive" cooperation with the weapons inspection regime, although outstanding issues remained. Blix added that while Iraqi cooperation had not been "immediate" or "complete," as required in UN Security Council resolution 1441, neither was it entirely dilatory. In fact according to the UN News Center, on March 7, 2003, Blix told the Security Council that it would take "not years . . . but months" to resolve the key remaining disarmament tasks, promising to deliver such a plan to the Council before the end of this month. Twelve days later, the United States attacked.

Among all the explanations given for the Iraq War, we cannot ignore simple greed as a motive for this rash and ultimately catastrophic decision. Before joining George W. Bush's presidential ticket in 2000, Dick Cheney spent 16 years as CEO of the oilfield services behemoth Halliburton Company, where—with no business experience to speak of—he landed after serving as secretary of defense for Bush's father, George H. W. Bush. In the first weeks of his vice presidency, Cheney convened the National Energy Policy Development Group, whose charge was to develop a national energy policy for the United States. Its deliberations—attended primarily by top executives of major oil companies (who later denied this to Congress)—were held in complete secret. Documents shaken free by a Freedom of Information Act suit filed by Judicial Watch and the Sierra Club showed that as early as March 2001—months before the 9/11 attacks—the energy task force members were already planning to profit from Iraqi oil fields. Nor did Cheney forget his friends at Halliburton. The energy giant's spin-off, KBR, received a better-than-1,000-to-1 return on the $34 million severance package it handed Cheney, when KBR was awarded $39.5 billion in US government contracts in Iraq, making them the top defense contractor of that disastrous war.

Those Elusive Weapons of Mass Destruction

In May 2004, a little over a year after the invasion, President George W. Bush put on a light-hearted slide show at the annual Radio and Television Correspondents Dinner in Washington. In one of the images, he was seen searching for something under the furniture in the Oval Office. "Those weapons of mass destruction have got to be here somewhere," he joked. "Nope, no weapons over there," he chuckled as he clicked on another slide. "Maybe under here?" As it happened, Saddam Hussein's weapons of mass destruction program was just as likely to be found in the White House as in Iraq. Most of Saddam's stockpiles of chemical and biological weapons had been destroyed under UN supervision after the Gulf War. And despite the Bush administration's insistence that the Iraqi regime was still producing WMDs, there was no such program in operation.

Bush's performance at the Correspondents Dinner made a horrifying joke of a rather serious public relations problem plaguing his administration: one of his two rationales for attacking Iraq had turned out to be false. (The other—that Saddam Hussein bore responsibility for the attacks of 9/11—was also false.) In their memoirs, both George W. Bush and Dick Cheney insist that the failure to find weapons of mass destruction was the result of bad intelligence and honest mistakes. Both were happy to blame the CIA for providing erroneous information, quoting then-director George Tenet's guarantee that tying Saddam to such weapons was "a slam dunk." In fact, the CIA came under strong pressure from Bush and Cheney to provide the damning intelligence about Saddam that the administration eagerly sought during the run-up to the war.

The Bush administration often cited Saddam's "stock-piles" of chemical and biological weapons, but they found even more rhetorical power in evoking the threat of nuclear attack. Nuclear bombs are the quintessential weapon of mass destruction. They are the world-ending technology that haunts everyone who remembers Hiroshima and Nagasaki, or anyone who shivered through six decades of Cold War. In any ethical calculus, preventing a nuclear attack appears to justify any action short of launching one.

The war's planners used two insubstantial props to support their argument that Iraq was developing nuclear weapons: the yellowcake uranium Iraq supposedly sought from the African nation of Niger and the thousands of aluminum tubes Iraq ordered from Australia through a company in Jordan. Bush invoked both of these in his 2003 State of the Union address, telling the nation, "The British government has learned that Saddam Hussein recently sought significant quantities of uranium from Africa. Our intelligence sources tell us that he has attempted to purchase high-strength aluminum tubes suitable for nuclear weapons production."

The yellowcake story is particularly convoluted. Readers interested in following its entire peregrination from Italian spies to British government intrigue may wish to take a look at Craig Unger's 2006 piece on the subject in *Vanity Fair*. In brief, several obviously forged documents emerged suggesting that Saddam Hussein had attempted to arrange an annual purchase of five-hundred tons of partially processed uranium ore (known as yellowcake) from Niger. In his article, Unger summed up the problems with the documents:

> The forged documents were full of errors. A letter dated October 10, 2000, was signed by [Niger] Minister of Foreign Affairs Allele Elhadj Habibou—even though

he had been out of office for more than a decade. Its September 28 postmark indicated that somehow the letter had been received nearly two weeks before it was sent. In another letter, [Niger] President Tandja Mamadou's signature appeared to be phony. The accord signed by him referred to the Niger constitution of May 12, 1965, when a new constitution had been enacted in 1999. One of the letters was dated July 30, 1999, but referred to agreements that were not made until a year later. Finally, the agreement called for the 500 tons of uranium to be transferred from one ship to another in international waters—a spectacularly difficult feat.

State Department analysts doubted that the documents were genuine, but at Donald Rumsfeld's Defense Department, things were different. The Defense Intelligence Agency issued a "finished intelligence product," according to Unger, "titled 'Niamey [Niger's capital city] Signed an Agreement to Sell 500 Tons of Uranium a Year to Baghdad,'" and gave it to Dick Cheney's office. Cheney tasked the CIA, whose analysts disagreed among themselves about the likelihood of the claim, with digging further. The request landed on CIA officer Valerie Plame's desk, and she asked her husband Joseph C. Wilson to look into it. Wilson had been George H. W. Bush's ambassador to nearby Gabon and was familiar with Niger's political landscape. Wilson returned from Niger with the news that there was no evidence of an Iraqi attempt to buy uranium. In July 2003, much to the annoyance of Vice President Cheney, Wilson published an op-ed in the *New York Times,* called "What I Didn't Find in Africa."

Cheney got his revenge that same month, when syndicated Washington columnist Robert Novak revealed that

Plame worked for the CIA. The leaked information came from Cheney's chief of staff, Lewis "Scooter" Libby, who was later convicted of lying to a grand jury investigating the charges and sentenced to thirty months in federal prison. But Libby ended up serving less than a month behind bars. Declaring that the damage to Libby's professional reputation was sufficient punishment, and facing what he called in his memoir *Decision Points* an "agonizing decision," President Bush intervened to commute his sentence.

In the years since the invasion, Bush and Cheney have sought to minimize the importance of their claim that Saddam was seeking uranium from Niger. In his memoir, Bush refers to the flat declaration in his 2003 State of the Union address that he had learned from the British that Saddam "recently sought significant quantities of uranium from Africa" as "those sixteen words." He seems perplexed that this "single sentence in my five-thousand-word speech . . . became a political controversy and a massive distraction." He also maintains that the Niger uranium "incident" was "not a major point in the case against Saddam."

Cheney's memoir also uses the phrase "sixteen words" more than once when discussing the 2003 State of the Union speech, but unlike Bush, he still wants his audience to think there might have been something to the Niger story after all. The CIA had told him a year before, writes Cheney, that "Iraq had existing stockpiles of yellowcake, or unenriched uranium ore, two hundred tons of which had previously been acquired from Niger, but that these stockpiles were in sealed containers that the International Atomic Energy Agency inspected annually." He found this "interesting," because it meant that "if Saddam intended to restart his nuclear program, he was going to have to acquire uranium clandestinely." In other words, the uranium Saddam *did* have was under IAEA lock and key, and by early 2003 the adminis-tration knew that the Niger story was false, which made the whole nuclear threat—by Cheney's own logic—considerably less likely. Yet the drumbeat went on.

A forgery as clumsy as the Niger documents should not have convinced anyone. The question remains to this day: were Bush, Rumsfeld and Cheney being played, or were they playing the rest of the world?

The aluminum tubes are a different story. Unlike uranium from Niger, it seems that Saddam Hussein was indeed trying to acquire them and continued trying after the first shipment was interdicted in Jordan. The question is, what did he want them for? The CIA argued that the tubes were to become the rotating arms of a gas centrifuge, used to produce enriched uranium for a nuclear weapon.

One Sunday in September 2002, Scooter Libby leaked this classified "information" to Michael R. Gordon and Judith Miller, who published an uncritical story in the *New York Times*. Now the nation's "newspaper of record" was on record that Iraq was trying to make a bomb. That same day, a crew of top administration officials representing the White House, the Defense Department, the State Department, and the National Security Council—including Dick Cheney, Colin Powell, Donald Rumsfeld, Condoleezza Rice, and General Richard Myers, chairman of the Joint Chiefs of Staff—made the rounds of the Sunday talk shows. They were all selling the same story: Saddam was making a bomb, and the aluminum tubes proved it.

But there was no such proof. Both the US Department of Energy and the State Department's Bureau of Intelligence Research concluded the tubes would most likely be used for conventional artillery rockets, and this information appeared in a National Intelligence Estimate, whose summary George

W. Bush saw in October 2002. The CIA disagreed with this analysis, but DOE and the Bureau of Intelligence Research turned out to be right.

Despite their flimsy and contrived evidence, the Bush war planners were not shy about using the nuclear threat to promote military action against Iraq. A year before the invasion, in March 2002, Cheney told CNN that Saddam "is actively pursuing nuclear weapons at this time." In a televised address in October of that same year, President Bush first used the metaphor that would come to represent the whole ball of confabulation rolled out to justify the Iraq war. "Facing clear evidence of peril," he told the American people, "we cannot wait for the final proof—the smoking gun—that could come *in the form of a mushroom cloud* [emphasis added]."

The next month, National Security Advisor Condoleezza Rice used the same phrase in an interview with CNN's Wolf Blitzer. "The problem here," said Rice, "is that there will always be some uncertainty about how quickly [Saddam Hussein] can acquire nuclear weapons. But we don't want the smoking gun to be a mushroom cloud."

In February 2003, Secretary of State Colin Powell made the US case for war in a speech to the UN Security Council, a speech now famous primarily for the amount of false information it contained. After discussing evidence that Iraq held stockpiles of chemical and biological weapons, Powell once again reminded the world, "Saddam Hussein is determined to get his hands on a nuclear bomb," and pointed to the aluminum tubes as evidence. Finally, on March 16, 2003, four days before the invasion, Cheney appeared on NBC's *Meet the Press* and told the hosts that Saddam "has been absolutely devoted to trying to acquire nuclear weapons. And we believe he has, in fact, reconstituted nuclear weapons."

Two months later, when none of these "reconstituted" weapons had turned up, Defense Secretary Rumsfeld told a Senate Subcommittee on Appropriations point blank, "I don't believe anyone that I know in the administration ever said that Iraq had nuclear weapons."

How Many Have Died in the Iraq War?

When asked about casualties of American bombing in Afghanistan, General Tommy Franks, head of the US Central Command, famously told reporters, "You know, we don't do body counts." Nor does the US government provide "body counts" for the Iraq war. Fortunately, other people do.

Estimates of deaths in the Iraq War are not hard to come by. Evaluating them is a bit trickier. For one thing, different studies have measured different kinds of deaths. Some have counted only violent deaths. Others have focused on the entire number of "excess deaths"—that is, the number of deaths exceeding those predicted by pre-war death rates. On the high end are two studies by researchers at Johns Hopkins University published in the respected British medical journal the *Lancet* and one by a British polling agency called Opinion Research Business International. The first *Lancet* study, published in 2004, estimated roughly 98,000 excess deaths as a result of the invasion, not including deaths in the embattled city of Fallujah. (Data from Fallujah was excluded so as not to skew the results because death rates there were so much higher than in Iraq as a whole.) The report estimated an additional 200,000 deaths in the area of Fallujah alone.

Equally important as the sheer numbers is the *kind* of death the *Lancet* reported. Prior to the invasion, the leading causes of death in Iraq were heart attacks and strokes. After the invasion, according to the *Lancet*, violence was responsible for somewhere between 24 and 51 percent of all deaths, depending on whether or not the Fallujah data was included.

Two years later, the *Lancet* published a second study that estimated that 654,965 more Iraqis had died than would have done so before the war, 601,027 of whom died as a result of violence, most commonly by gunfire.

In September 2007, the consulting firm Opinion Research Business International published the highest estimate of combined deaths of civilians and combatants—a staggering 1.2 million. The ORB report, which was based on survey results from about 1,500 Iraqi adults in fifteen of the eighteen Iraqi states, generated tremendous controversy over both its methodology and its conclusions, and most observers believe it to be an over-estimate.

On the lower side are the figures provided by Iraqi Body Count, a British non-governmental organization that keeps a running tally of deaths reported in the news media and from other government and NGO sources such as morgues and hospitals. IBC says it "records the violent deaths that have resulted from the 2003 military intervention in Iraq" that are "caused by US-led coalition and Iraqi government forces and paramilitary or criminal attacks." Unlike the numbers from the Johns Hopkins and ORB studies, the IBC's figure is not an estimate based on polling. It is a direct count of reported violent deaths. By necessity it is an undercount; it is inconceivable that IBC's sources could capture every violent death. As of July 2015, the IBC's Iraq Body Count stood at 216,000 for combatants and civilians combined. The figure for civilians alone ranges between 140,563 and 159,127.

By any count, too many people have died in an illegal and preventable war.

It Doesn't Matter Whether Saddam Had Weapons of Mass Destruction

The fact that Bush administration officials used false and distorted evidence to justify their invasion of Iraq makes their decision all the more deplorable. But in the end, it doesn't matter whether or not Saddam Hussein had warehouses full of WMDs—the war in Iraq would still have been a crime against peace and a violation of the laws and customs of war. And Bush and his war council could still be charged as war criminals.

As early as September 2004, then-UN Secretary General Kofi Annan told the BBC that the invasion and occupation of Iraq was a war "not in conformity with the UN charter from our point of view." In fact, he acknowledged, "From the charter point of view, it was illegal." Annan was referring to Article 2 of the UN charter, which states in part, "All Members shall refrain in their international relations from the threat or use of force against the territorial integrity or political independence of any state."

Article 51 of the UN charter does guarantee a nation's right to self-defense "if an armed attack occurs." Article 51 says nothing about preemptive self-defense absent an armed attack. However, preemptive self-defense is a principle that has long been recognized in international law. A nation need not wait until it is actually attacked, but the certainty that an attack is coming must be "instant, overwhelming, and leaving no choice of means," as then-Secretary of State Daniel Webster wrote to the British government in 1837. (In the course of putting down a rebellion in Canada, the British had claimed self-defense when they captured and burned an American ship they suspected of being involved in gun-running for the Canadians.) Webster's insistence that a threat be "instant, overwhelming, and leaving no choice of means" remains the *de facto* standard for legitimate preemptive self-defense.

In March 2003, it simply was not the case that the United States faced a danger that was "instant, overwhelming, and leaving no choice of means"—even if Iraq were in possession of the weapons the Bush administration claimed it had. On the other hand, during that spring there certainly *was* one nation facing a determined, powerful, even nuclear-armed enemy—a nation threatened with the "instant, overwhelming" danger of attack. But it wasn't the United States or one of its allies. It was Iraq. Given that the United States made no secret of its intentions or its military preparations, would Iraq have been justified (assuming it had the capacity) in attacking the United States?

The view that preemptive self-defense is only legitimate *in extremis* is at odds with a September 2002 Bush administration document titled "The National Security Strategy of the

United States," which is often described as the best official formulation of the so-called Bush Doctrine. Arguing that the "security environment confronting the United States today is radically different from what we have faced before," the document outlined a new strategy in which the government's "first duty" is as always "to protect the American people and American interests." Therefore,

> [t]he United States has long maintained the option of preemptive actions to counter a sufficient threat to our national security. The greater the threat, the greater is the risk of inaction— and the more compelling the case for taking anticipatory action to defend ourselves, *even if uncertainty remains as to the time and place of the enemy's attack* [emphasis added]. To forestall or prevent such hostile acts by our adversaries, the United States will, if necessary, act preemptively.

In his memoir, *Decision Points,* Bush describes the elaboration of his "doctrine" this way:

> After 9/11, I developed a strategy to protect the country that came to be known as the Bush Doctrine: First, make no distinction between the terrorists and the nations that harbor them—and hold both to account. Second, take the fight to the enemy overseas before they can attack us again here at home. Third, confront threats before they fully materialize. And fourth, advance liberty and hope as an alternative to the enemy's ideology of repression and fear.

The doctrine that there is "no distinction" between terrorists and the country where they are located underlay the argument for the war against Afghanistan, and the administration intended to apply the same doctrine to its attack on Iraq. That is why they were quite willing to use torture to extract statements from detainees "proving" that Saddam Hussein had conspired with al Qaeda.

In fact, Bush officials were prepared to deploy a number of arguments for the war. The problem they had, as Paul Wolfowitz later told *Vanity Fair,* was deciding which argument would be most effective. "The truth is," he said, "that for reasons that have a lot to do with the US government bureaucracy, we settled on the one issue that everyone could agree on, which was weapons of mass destruction as the core reason." This is a rather startling statement, which Wolfowitz attempted to clarify, explaining that "there have always been three fundamental concerns. One is weapons of mass destruction, the second is support for terrorism, the third is the criminal treatment of the Iraqi people." The third issue, he said was "a reason to help the Iraqis but . . . not a reason to put American kids' lives at risk." (Or presumably, the lives of hundreds of thousands of Iraqis.) "That second issue about links to terrorism is the one about which there's the most disagreement within the bureaucracy," Wolfowitz continued. So that left the Bush administration with only the (nonexistent) weapons of mass destruction as a pretext for war.

So the Bush administration began telling the US public and the world that Saddam Hussein possessed weapons that could kill thousands, and that his government represented "a direct and growing threat" to the United States. Neither of these things was true. Iraq posed no direct and imminent threat to the United States. Therefore, the US invasion of Iraq was, as Kofi Annan stated, illegal.

But didn't the UN Security Council tacitly approve military action against Iraq when it passed Security Council Resolution 1441? This was last of several resolutions requiring Iraq to comply with weapons inspections by the United Nations Monitoring, Verification and Inspection Commission (UNMOVIC) and the International Atomic Energy Agency (IAEA). Some proponents of the Iraq War have made that argument. However, the US ambassador to the United Nations at the time, John Negroponte, sought to dispel exactly those fears that the United States would interpret the resolution as a license for war. In the discussions before the vote, Negroponte assured the Security Council, "This resolution contains no 'hidden triggers' and no 'automaticity' with respect to the use of force. If there is a further Iraqi breach, reported to the Council by UNMOVIC, the IAEA or a Member State, the matter will return to the Council for discussions." The British ambassador used almost identical words to reassure the Security Council that before attacking Iraq, the United States and Britain would seek the Security Council's blessing.

That is not what happened, however. On February 24, 2003, Washington and London did bring a resolution for war to the Security Council, but it became apparent that two permanent members, France and Russia, would veto it if it came to a vote. Meeting with British Prime Minister Tony Blair and the presidents of Spain and Portugal, Bush decided to withdraw the resolution. "We all agreed," he wrote in his memoir, that "the diplomatic track had reached its end."

The Other Superpower

Not only did members of the Security Council oppose the US march to war, so did most of the world. Writing in the *Nation* at the start of the war, distinguished journalist Jonathan Schell called the peoples of the earth "the other superpower." He described the international repugnance and outrage at the Bush administration's drive to war:

> A new phenomenon of rolling demonstrations circled the world—not only in the great capitals but also in provincial cities and even small towns . . . . Most newspapers outside the United States opposed the war. UN Secretary General Kofi Annan expressed his chagrin. The Pope said the war "threatens the destiny of humanity." For once, the majority of the world's governments spoke up unequivocally for the majorities of their peoples.

Public opinion polls, observed Schell, "showed that in most countries opposition to the war was closer to unanimity than to a mere majority."

Tragically, of course, "the other superpower" failed to hold back the US juggernaut. But perhaps the force of world opinion can now bring those responsible for the war to justice.

Sadly, the US Congress was not part of this "other superpower." In the Iraq War Resolution passed in October 2002, Congress gave President Bush permission to use the US armed forces "as he determines to be necessary and appropriate" to "defend the national security of the United States against the continuing threat posed by Iraq; and enforce all relevant United Nations Security Council Resolutions regarding Iraq." The vote in the House was 297 to 133. In the Senate it was 77 to 23. Those who stood up to the administration, even those with secure seats, showed genuine courage at a time when the country seemed hell-bent on war and misdirected revenge.

Many of those who voted for the war, including prominent senators like Democrats Jay Rockefeller and Hillary Rodham Clinton, now say they would have opposed it, had they known that the administration was lying about the danger Iraq posed. One could argue that those political leaders who belatedly (and safely) expressed their regrets should have been more suspicious of the administration's claims at the time. Certainly there was plenty of evidence for doubt that was easily available during the run-up to war.

But in evaluating the criminality of the Bush administration warmakers, none of this matters. Even if every word that Bush, Cheney, Rumsfeld, Rice, Wolfowitz, *et al.* said had been true, the war would still have been illegal.

Of course, Congress and the top officials of the Bush administration are not the only ones to blame for clamoring for war. What about the American people? To what extent should we hold ourselves responsible for the crime of waging an aggressive war against Iraq? The Allies considered a similar question when planning the Nuremberg tribunals. They tried the high Nazi officials they could lay their hands on at the first Nuremberg trial, and later, quite a few at lower levels of responsibility as well. They also instituted a process of "de-Nazification" to prevent former party members from holding government office in Germany.*

But the Allies never intended to prosecute the entire German people for starting World War II. There is an

---

* Many war criminals slipped through this screening process, including prominent Nazis like Hans Globke, who helped write the infamous Nuremberg laws that defined who was a Jew, and Reinhard Gehlen, Hitler's spymaster on the Eastern front. Globke became West German Chancellor Konrad Adenauer's indispensable chief of staff after the war, and Gehlen became West Germany's powerful intelligence chief.

important difference between Germany and the United States, however. Under the Nazis, Germany was an explicitly totalitarian state, in which all authority derived directly from the *Fuhrer*, Adolph Hitler. The United States, on the other hand, is at least nominally a democracy with a government "deriving [its] just powers from the consent of the governed," in the words of the Declaration of Independence. To what extent did the governed of this nation consent to the Iraq war?

We can find some answers in polling data. In March 2003, a Gallup poll showed that 75 percent of the US public believed it was "not a mistake" to send troops to Iraq. By June of 2015 that number had dropped to 46 percent—still a large minority. Those who now believe it was a mistake represent a bare majority—51 percent.

But is it fair to blame the American people for Bush administration machinations? After all, if politically sophisticated members of Congress were fooled, how can we expect ordinary people to have seen through the administration's propaganda campaign—a campaign that was widely aided by the media (and not just by Fox News, but in some cases by "liberal" media organizations like the *New York Times*)? At what point does the failure to know—that a war is illegal or that people are being tortured—become more than foolish ignorance? When does it become culpable?

I think that the war on terror has eroded in the people of this country the quality that is sometimes called practical wisdom. Practical wisdom is an intellectual habit we develop over time, one that allows a person to examine a situation and understand its moral contours. It is a habit of thought that helps us understand in a given situation what are the right things to do and the right ways to do them. Practical wisdom requires another habit—courage—if we are to look

91

squarely at the world. We need to not only sift through the media babble that constantly assaults and misleads us as we seek the truth, but also to question our own emotions and biases that inevitably arise in times of national crisis.

I believe that after a decade and a half of constant "terror manipulation"—relentless messaging about the dangers that lurk all around us, particularly those involving Muslims and brown-skinned people—we have been damaged morally. In the name of security, we have been terrorized by our own government—and by the news and entertainment corporations that feed on exploiting such fear—into giving up not only our own freedoms but our fundamental sense of human empathy. While racist contempt for "foreigners" has long been a feature of the American psyche, years of terror propaganda and "security theater" have created something qualitatively different. Entire swaths of the world's population are now regarded as enemies by many American people, seen as vicious, less-than-human creatures who are undeserving of basic decency, let alone the protection of international law.

As a nation, we need to reclaim these qualities of wisdom and courage. Facing the terrible crimes that have been committed in our names and bringing the criminals to justice would be a good beginning. It would help restore not only the rule of international law, but our own humanity.

War! What Is It Good for?

Of course, not all observers believe that war is always a bad thing. In many people's view, war provides a necessary winnowing tool, useful for distinguishing between predators and sheep and for keeping the former's teeth sharp. The German philosopher Georg Hegel believed that war refined the state that practiced it, offering individual people the opportunity to freely bind themselves to the state through sacrifice of property and even their lives. "War is not to be regarded as an absolute evil," wrote Hegel. In fact, "successful wars have checked domestic unrest and consolidated the power of the state at home." War is good for a country; like a wind that blows over stagnant waters, it eliminates the "corruption in nations" that "would be the product of a prolonged, let alone 'perpetual' peace." Readers may not be surprised to learn that Hegel's views on the relationship between the individual and the state and the value of war were popular among Nazi ideologues.

Lest Americans think we've outgrown this bit of Hegelian dialectic, remember that many pundits criticized the Bush administration not for making war against Iraq but for doing it in such a way that most people in this country had no sacrifices to make.

The former war correspondent Chris Hedges has addressed the appeal of war as a refining fire for individual human lives. He recognized the profound, even addictive, emotional power of living with danger in the service of some transcendent cause. In *War Is a Force that Gives Us Meaning*, Hedges describes how the adrenaline-fueled urgency of war gives us permission to forget the responsibilities of daily life in service of a greater duty. In war our lives, our sacrifices, all our actions take on a transcendent meaning. But Hedges warns that this feeling is seductively powerful, that its ecstasies make us unfit us for ordinary life, for ordinary joys and sorrows. And in the end, don't we say we are fighting wars in order to restore the possibility of ordinary life?

Like Hedges, in a small way I've felt the seductive attraction of war. In 1984 I spent six months working in the Nicaraguan war zones with an organization called Witness for Peace. My job was to interview survivors of attacks by the contras, the counter-revolutionary forces supported—at that time illegally—by the Reagan administration. I remember lying in bed one night in the mining town of Siuna, listening to the boom of mortars falling somewhere not too far away. I remember wishing the sound would come closer, that the danger would come nearer, because that would be more thrilling. That's when I knew it was time for me to do what the Nicaraguans couldn't do. It was time for me to leave the war and go home.

Waging an aggressive war is the original war crime from which all other war crimes spring. We'll look at some of these other crimes committed by US officials after 9/11 in the next chapter.

Table of Principal Bush Administration Officials Responsible for Crimes against Peace

Name	Position
Elliott Abrams	National Security Council Senior Director for Democracy, Human Rights, and International Operations : June 25, 2001—December 1, 2002 National Security Council Senior Director for Near East and North African Affairs: December 2, 2002—February 1, 2005 Deputy National Security Advisor for Global Democracy Strategy: February 2, 2005—January 2009
Richard Armitage	US Deputy Secretary of State: March 26, 2001—February 22, 2005
John Bolton	Assistant Secretary of State for Arms Control and International Security: May 11, 2001—July 31, 2005 US Ambassador to the United Nations (never confirmed in office): August 1, 2005—December 9, 2006
George W. Bush	US President: January 20, 2001—January 20, 2009
Dick Cheney	Vice President: January 20, 2001—January 20, 2009
Douglas Feith	Under Secretary of Defense for Policy: July 2001—August 2005
Zalmay Khalilzad	U. S. Ambassador to Afghanistan: November 28, 2003—June 20, 2005 US Ambassador to Iraq: June 21, 2005—April 17, 2007 US Ambassador to the United Nations: April 17, 2007—January 20, 2009

Name	Position
Richard Myers	Chairman of the Joint Chiefs of Staff: October 1, 2001—September 30, 2005
John Negroponte	US Ambassador to the United Nations (G.W. Bush): September 15, 2001– April 2004 US Ambassador to Iraq: May 6, 2004—April 2005 US Director of National Intelligence: April 21, 2005—February 13, 2007 US Deputy Secretary of State: February 13, 2007—January 20, 2009
Richard Perle	Chairman, Defense Policy Board Advisory Committee: 2001–2003
Colin Powell	US Secretary of State: January 20, 2001—January 26, 2005
Condoleezza Rice	US National Security Advisor: January 20, 2001—January 26, 2005 US Secretary of State: January 26, 2005—January 20, 2009
Donald Rumsfeld	US Secretary of Defense: January 20, 2001—December 18, 2006
George Tenet	Director of Central Intelligence: December 15, 1996—July 11, 2004
Paul Wolfowitz	US Deputy Secretary of Defense: January 20, 2001—June 1, 2005

Chapter 4

War Crimes

After years of disclosures by government investigations, media accounts, and reports from human rights organizations, there is no longer any doubt as to whether the [Bush] administration has committed war crimes. The only question that remains to be answered is whether those who ordered the use of torture will be held to account.

— Maj. General (Ret.) Anthony Taguba, June 2008

If you don't violate someone's human rights some of the time, you probably aren't doing your job.

—Anonymous US official speaking to the
Washington Post in Afghanistan, December 2002

War crimes are violations of the laws and customs of war. They are also crimes of "universal jurisdiction," which means that any nation has the right, even the duty, to prosecute alleged war criminals, or to make them available for extradition so they can be prosecuted somewhere else. This universal jurisdiction over war crimes arises from a concept that international law calls *jus cogens,* or "compelling law." The international community considers some actions taken during war—rape, torture, exterminations, forced expulsions, extrajudicial killing, use of forbidden weapons—to be so terrible that every country is compelled to prosecute them whenever they occur.

The United States has certainly committed war crimes in the context of the war on terror, but not every outrage of that "war" qualifies as a *war* crime. As I've argued, the Bush administration used the term "war on terror" to refer to many activities that fall outside the sort of widespread and sustained armed conflict that constitutes a true war. However, the United States has fought two *genuine* wars within the war on terror—in Afghanistan and Iraq. In that context, officials at the highest levels of US government as well as many in the next ranks, along with quite a few private contractors, have in fact committed war crimes. These include violations of the Geneva Conventions, of the US War Crimes Act, and of domestic and international prohibitions on the use of chemical weapons.

US war crimes committed since 9/11 are numerous and varied. They include actions taken in two countries, conducted over more than a decade, and under the aegis of several different US government authorities, including the regular armed services, the Joint Special Operations Command (JSOC), the Department of Defense (including the Defense Intelligence Agency, or DIA), the CIA, the White House, and the National Security Council, among others.

While most Americans are familiar with the CIA, and many have heard of the DIA, until recently JSOC's place in the

US arsenal has remained relatively unknown. Each branch of the US armed forces has its own divisions devoted to the missions that require special skills and employ unconventional warfare. Such missions are called "special operations." In the Navy, SEALS are responsible for special ops. The Marines have the Marine Raiders. Army Special Forces soldiers are known as Green Berets. The Air Force uses the straightforward title US Air Force Special Forces. Historically, these special forces have reported to USSOCOM, the US Special Operations Command. But within USSOCOM, there is another agency, the Joint Special Operations Command, or JSOC, whose official mission is counterterrorism and whose activities are highly classified. Even the rest of USSOCOM doesn't know exactly what this shadowy unit does. As Jeremy Scahill has written in *Dirty Wars: The World Is a Battlefield,* "When a president of the United States want[s] to conduct an operation in total secrecy, away from the prying eyes of Congress, the best bet [is] not the CIA, but rather JSOC."

Many of the crimes described in this chapter involve torture and other mistreatment of detainees. Some of the people the United States has imprisoned in the war on terror were and, in the case of those who still haven't been released, continue to be prisoners of war under the Geneva Convention Three. These include any members of the Afghan armed forces under the Taliban government and any Iraqi soldiers serving under Saddam Hussein. Others, including detainees accused of being members of al Qaeda or other non-state entities, qualify for the lesser but still life-saving protections that Geneva Convention Four provides for civilians who have been captured during a war. Prisoners who were captured outside Afghanistan but brought to US-run facilities in Afghanistan should also be protected under Geneva, because the United States was involved in a shooting war in that country, and Afghanistan, like the United States, is a party to the Geneva Conventions. Finally, many of those detained in Afghanistan or Iraq were not involved in the conflict in any way but were simply sold to the United States for bounties or were victims of mistaken identity. They, too, deserve the protections of Geneva Four.

Violations of the Geneva Conventions are war crimes under international law. People accused of war crimes can be tried in the International Criminal Court—*if* they are citizens of a country that has signed the treaty creating the court. The United States did sign the original treaty, but it was never ratified by the US Senate. In fact, as we have seen, in May 2002 the Bush administration withdrew its signature. Defense Secretary Rumsfeld issued his explanation for the withdrawal, stating that

> the ICC provisions claim the authority to detain and try American citizens—US soldiers, sailors, airmen and Marines, *as well as current and future officials* [emphasis added]—even though the United States has not given its consent to be bound by the treaty. When the ICC treaty enters into force this summer, U.S. citizens will be exposed to the risk of prosecution by a court that is unaccountable to the American people, and that has no obligation to respect the Constitutional rights of our citizens.

Even if Bush and Rumsfeld succeeded in keeping "current and future officials" out of an international tribunal, in fact, many high-ranking US officials could still be brought into court to answer for war crimes—to US federal court, that is. The 1996 War Crimes Act defines federal war crimes offenses, including any "grave breach" of the four 1949 Geneva Conventions or of Common Article 3 (covering non-international con-flicts). The federal war crimes law goes on to list the kind of actions that constitute a grave breach of Geneva: torture, cruel or inhuman treatment, performing biological experiments, murder, mutilation or maiming, intentionally causing serious bodily injury, rape, sexual assault or abuse, and taking hostages. As we shall see, many actions sanctioned by US officials at the very highest level are punishable under the War Crimes Act. It is worth noting that there is no statute of limitations for these war crimes.

The War Crimes Act also covers violations of certain provisions of the 1907 Hague Convention Respecting the Law and Custom of War on Land. One of these is found in Article 23(e), which makes it unlawful "[t]o employ arms, projectiles, or material calculated to cause unnecessary suffering." This section of the act is relevant because, as we shall see, it is very likely that in the war in Iraq, the United States did in fact use weapons "calculated to cause unnecessary suffering."

In order to bring some organization to a wide-ranging discussion, I've divided this chapter geographically, first considering detention practices in Afghanistan and then in Iraq. After looking at how the United States has treated its prisoners in the wars in Afghanistan and Iraq, we'll consider another violation of the laws and customs of war: the use of chemical weapons, in particular white phosphorus, in Iraq, which may well be a violation of the 1907 Hague Convention.

Afghanistan

In the years since the United States attacked Afghanistan in October 2001, at least three US authorities have detained prisoners there: the CIA, the DIA, and JSOC. All of them have abused detainees, and in many cases, tortured them.

For some prisoners, Afghanistan was a way station between their place of capture and rendition for torture and interrogation in Morocco, Egypt, Syria, or some other accommodating country. For others, it was a stop-over on the way to Guantánamo. For at least two detainees, it was the end of the line.

Deaths in custody: In December 2002, two men died in US military custody at the Bagram Collection Point (later renamed the Bagram Theater Internment Facility). As is common in Afghanistan, both men went by single names: Dilawar and Habibullah. Dilawar's story is chronicled in the documentary film *Taxi to the Dark Side* and mentioned in Chapter 1. The two men died within days of each other, and their similar stories demonstrate that their treatment formed part of a larger pattern of abuse at Bagram. Habibullah was a mullah (a learned Muslim) and the brother of a Taliban leader, although there's no evidence that he himself was involved in hostilities against the US-led forces in Afghanistan. Dilawar was an Afghan taxi driver, who was arrested at a checkpoint along with the three passengers in his cab. Those three spent 15 months in Guantánamo, although they were never charged with any crime. The *New York Times* reported in 2005 that "[t]he three passengers in Mr. Dilawar's taxi were sent home from Guantánamo in March 2004, 15 months after their capture, with letters saying they posed 'no threat' to American forces."

For days, US soldiers shackled both Dilawar and Habibullah by their ankles and wrists, arms above their heads, and beat them repeatedly, using a method called "peroneal strikes." This is a punitive technique that involves hitting or kneeing the peroneal nerve, which lies right below the knee joint. Peroneal strikes cause unbearable nerve pain and, with repeated infliction, permanent nerve damage.

In the two men's case, permanent nerve damage wasn't an issue, because both died within a few days of their capture—Habibullah from a "[p]ulmonary embolism due to blunt force injury to the legs." In other words, he was beaten so hard that a clot formed inside a blood vessel in his leg, traveled to his lungs, and killed him.

New York Times reporter Carlotta Gall broke the story of the two deaths in 2004. Gall wrote that the Army had charged James P. Boland, "a reserve military police soldier from Cincinnati," with assault and recommended charges against "two dozen" other low-level soldiers, many of whom were later acquitted or given light sentences. No one of higher rank was prosecuted. Those not charged include Army Captain Carolyn Wood, who was the head of interrogations at the Bagram Collection Point, and was later transferred to Abu Ghraib prison in Iraq. Neither Wood nor any of her superior officers suffered any repercussions for these homicides at Bagram.

Dilawar and Habibullah were not the first prisoners in Afghanistan to die in US hands. Drawing on work by British investigative journalist Andy Worthington, a Washington-based think tank called the Constitution Project related an especially harrowing story in its 2013 report on detainee treatment. At the start of the Afghanistan War, somewhere between 1,100 and 13,000 Taliban soldiers were seized, "together with an unknown number of fleeing civilians," when they surrendered to Abdul Rashid Dostum, an Afghan militia leader allied with the US. For reasons that aren't entirely clear, Dostum sent two hundred of these prisoners on a three-hundred-mile journey from Yerghanek to Sheberghan in a shipping container. (During the Afghan civil war, commanders in both the Taliban and the Northern Alliance had murdered prisoners by packing them into shipping containers, so this was a familiar tactic.) Survivors of the trip told Constitution Project interviewers that when the container doors were opened, "the whole spectacle" was "illuminated by spotlights operated by US Special Forces soldiers." Of the two-hundred men packed into the container, only twenty were still alive. The others had suffocated. This is a war crime.

The role of US Special Forces in this incident "remains unclear" according to the Constitution Project because the incident itself was never investigated. However, it's not unreasonable to think that Special Forces expected the "delivery," since they were prepared with spotlights to receive the survivors. It is also unclear under whose command the Special Forces at Kandahar were operating. All Army Special Forces form part of the United States Special Operations Command, but only some are under the direct command of JSOC. If the Special Forces were working under JSOC, then their commander at the time bears responsibility. In 2001 this was Lieutenant General Dell L. Dailey. His better-known successors, Gens. Stanley McChrystal and William McRaven, didn't take over until 2003 and 2008 respectively. In 2009, President Obama promised an investigation into the Kandahar deaths, but to date no results of any inquiry have been released.

Detainee treatment in Afghanistan: At the beginning of the war, General Tommy Franks, then the commander of US Central Command, ordered US personnel in Afghanistan to observe the Geneva Conventions when handling prisoners. On January 19, 2002, according to the Constitution Project's report, Defense Secretary Donald Rumsfeld wrote to Franks, rescinding that order.

About two weeks later, on February 7, 2002, President Bush issued his memorandum (described in Chapter 2) to the same effect, stating that for a variety of reasons, neither

Taliban nor al Qaeda captives were covered under any of the four Geneva Conventions, including Common Article 3. Nevertheless, he said, "As a matter of policy, the United States Armed Forces shall continue to treat detainees humanely and, to the extent appropriate and consistent with military necessity, in a manner consistent with the principles of Geneva."

Bush based his February memorandum on another one from White House legal counsel Alberto Gonzales, dated January 25, 2002. (Gonzales would later replace John Ashcroft as Bush's attorney general.) This famous communication, signed by Gonzales, asserted that "the war against terrorism is a new kind of war," one which "renders obsolete Geneva's *strict limitations on questioning of enemy prisoners* [emphasis added] and renders quaint some of its provisions" such as commissary privileges. Not only would prisoners in the war on terror be denied commissary privileges, any limitations on how they might be "questioned" were also a "quaint" artifact of a bygone age. Although the memo carried Gonzales's signature, in 2007 the *Washington Post* reported that "[a] White House lawyer with direct knowledge said Cheney's lawyer, Addington, wrote the memo." The *Post* was referring to David Addington, then Dick Cheney's legal counsel in the office of the Vice President. Gonzales himself has acknowledged that Addington "contributed" to the memo.

In this same February 2002 memo, Bush also asserted that he accepted "the arguments of the Attorney General [then John Ashcroft] and the Justice Department" that he had "the authority under the Constitution to suspend Geneva as between the United States and Afghanistan," but, he said, "I decline to exercise that authority at this time." However, the memo continued, "I reserve the right to exercise the authority in this or future conflicts." In other words, Bush claimed the right as president to abrogate a signed and ratified international treaty, but in this case he had no need to invoke that right because none of the prisoners captured in Afghanistan were covered by Geneva anyway.

In 2006, the US Supreme Court decided differently. The court ruled in *Hamdan v. Rumsfeld* that a member of al Qaeda who was seized in Afghanistan and taken to Guantánamo *was* in fact covered by Geneva Common Article 3, which provides limited but important protection for prisoners seized in the context of a war that is not fought between two nations. In that decision, the justices declined to decide whether or not the petitioner, Salim Ahmed Hamdan, was eligible for protection under any *other* part of the Geneva Conventions because he fell under the protections of Common Article 3, which was all he needed for his petition to be granted. The justices thus declined to issue an opinion on whether al Qaeda prisoners were covered under any other part of the Conventions, such as Geneva Four, which provides protections for civilians who are detained during hostilities.

As we saw in Chapter 2, the Bush administration wanted to use a military commission to try Hamdan for conspiracy and terrorism. These commissions were set up, for reasons of "security," so that a defendant and his civilian lawyers could be removed from the courtroom during those parts of the testimony that the US prosecutors deemed "secret." For the same reason, neither Hamdan—who at one time had been Osama bin Laden's personal driver—nor his civilian lawyers would be allowed even to see all of the evidence presented against him. The Supreme Court decided that these procedures denied Hamdan the right, under Geneva Common Article 3, to be tried "by a regularly constituted court, affording all the judicial guarantees which are recognized as indispensable by civilized peoples."

What was so secret about the evidence and testimony Hamdan and his lawyers weren't allowed to see? In Hamdan's case, and in the cases of quite a few others, part of the government's problem was that the testimony against him had been produced by torture. Not only did this taint the quality of the evidence, but the Bush administration did not want specific torture methods revealed in open court. They were military secrets.

Bush's February 2002 memo requiring "humane treatment" of detainees referred only to constraints on the "US Armed Forces" and failed to mention other agencies such as the CIA. In order to be sure that Bush had not meant to include the spy agency in the directive about humane treatment, CIA Director George Tenet and the agency's general counsel at the time, Scott Muller, sought reassurance that their agency did indeed have a free hand with its prisoners. They wanted to know that they were not bound by Bush's February memo, and that no one was going to be charged with war crimes for what they were already doing to the prisoners in their control.

On February 12, 2003, Muller issued a memorandum "for the record," detailing the conversations with a variety of highly placed Bush administration officials that he had held in order to obtain this guarantee. Each official he spoke with had reassured him that the CIA was not bound by the Geneva Conventions, nor by the need to provide the "humane treatment" expected of the US military. Muller's memo is an excellent representation of the CIA's repeated attempts to secure approval—on the record—from administration officials for actions which they suspected were illegal.

First, some background: in the previous year, Deputy Attorney General John Yoo and Assistant Attorney General Jay Bybee had written two memos about detainee interrogation.

The two lawyers worked in the Justice Department's Office of Legal Counsel, which was responsible for providing legal advice to other parts of the executive branch, including the White House. One memo, addressed to Alberto Gonzales in his capacity as legal counsel to the president, was dated August 1, 2002. Its purpose was to interpret Section §2340 of the US Criminal Code, the "implementing legislation" passed by Congress to put the UN Convention against Torture into effect.

Gonzales was having trouble interpreting the act's definition of torture: "an act committed by a person acting under the color of law specifically intended to inflict severe physical or mental pain or suffering." As we saw in Chapter 2, Bybee provided an answer. "For an act to constitute torture as defined in Section 2340," he wrote, "it must inflict pain that is difficult to endure. Physical pain amounting to torture must be equivalent in intensity to the pain accompanying serious physical injury, such as organ failure, impairment of bodily function, or even death." On the same day, Bybee issued a second memo, approving specific methods—including waterboarding—to be used on a prisoner named Abu Zubaydah. (See Chapter 5.)

Now six months later, in February 2003, the CIA's Muller wanted to be sure that no one at the agency would be exposed to prosecution for war crimes as a result of the way they were treating prisoners. Members of the Bush administration had been making public statements to the effect that captured Taliban and al Qaeda suspects were being treated "humanely"—but Muller knew that, whether or not what the CIA was doing could be defined as torture according to the Justice Department guidelines, it certainly wasn't humane. His memo "for the record," recording his conversations with several key Bush administration officials, was clearly an attempt to establish legal cover for the CIA's interrogation methods. Muller's memo began by making it clear that many high-ranking Bush officials shared responsibility for the use of these "enhanced interrogation techniques," stating that they had been

> approved by the Attorney General [John Ashcroft] through the Office of Legal Counsel [at the Justice Department—including John Yoo and Jay Bybee] and carried on thereafter with the knowledge and concurrence of, among others, the Assistant Attorney General in charge of the Criminal Division [Deborah J. Daniels, now a managing partner at Krieg/Devault], the National Security Adviser [Condoleezza Rice], Counsel to the President [Alberto Gonzales], Counsel to the National Security Adviser, and Counsel to the Vice President [David Addington]. As of November 2002, others, including the General Counsel to the Department of Defense [William J. "Jim" Haynes II], were aware generally of the fact that CIA was authorized to conduct interrogations using techniques beyond those permitted under the Geneva conventions. No one ever suggested that there was any inconsistency between the authorized CIA conduct and the [president's] February Memo.

This was just the beginning of Muller's quest to ensure that higher-ups would share any blame that came the CIA's way. Next, Muller reported that he had discussed the matter with John Rizzo, who served as the CIA's acting general counsel until Muller took over. Rizzo assured Muller that "CIA use of interrogation techniques was *authorized by the President* [emphasis added]." In December 2002, Muller's memo continued, he had several conversations with John Yoo of the Justice Department's Office of Legal Counsel, who assured him that Bush's February 2002 memo did not apply to the CIA. In fact, Muller wrote, "Yoo stated that the language of the memorandum had been *deliberately limited* [emphasis added] to be binding only on 'the Armed Forces' which did not include the CIA." Yoo offered to send Muller "a written opinion to that effect." Muller had received a draft, but the final opinion was not yet in his hands when he wrote his report. Yoo further assured Muller that not only did the CIA's methods not violate the US law against torture (Section §2340), but they did not violate any other US law. It's likely that Yoo was thinking specifically of the 1996 War Crimes Act, although Muller's memo didn't say so.

In November 2002, Muller's memo went on, the Department of Defense handed over a prisoner to the CIA for interrogation, and asked CIA director Tenet to promise to return the prisoner when the agency was done with him. The DOD reminded Tenet of the president's memo requiring the armed forces to guarantee "humane treatment" of prisoners. But Muller sought reassurance from Jim Haynes, the DOD's general legal counsel, that while the prisoner was in CIA hands, there was no requirement to treat him humanely. Haynes reiterated what Yoo had told Muller before, that the president's memo only concerned the armed forces and did not apply to the CIA.

Muller recorded that on January 13, 2003, he attended a meeting at Alberto Gonzales's office—then serving as general counsel to the White House—along with David Addington, John Yoo, and Jim Haynes. The meeting was apparently convened to discuss a letter about detainee treatment that the DOD had received from Human Rights Watch. This time it was Addington and Haynes who confirmed that only the armed forces were legally required to treat detainees humanely.

Three days later, Muller attended a meeting with Condoleezza Rice, Donald Rumsfeld, Jim Haynes, Colin Powell, and Dick Cheney. Muller pointed out to Rice that the CIA had been authorized to do things that were inconsistent with "what at least some in the international community might expect in light of the Administration's public statements about 'humane treatment' of detainees."

As Muller's memo makes clear, the CIA had now received confirmation from the highest officials in the White House, the vice president's office, the National Security Council, the State Department, and the Department of Defense that it could do whatever it wanted with the prisoners it was holding. Nevertheless, half a year later, the CIA was again thrown into a tizzy when President Bush declared in his speech honoring the UN International Day in Support of Victims of Torture, "Torture anywhere is an affront to human dignity everywhere. The United States is committed to the worldwide elimination of torture, and we are leading this fight by example." The *Washington Post* story on the president's speech also carried a quote from Deputy White House Press Secretary Scott McClellan to the effect that all prisoners being held by the US government were being treated "humanely." John Rizzo, who was now the CIA's deputy general counsel, called John Bellinger, legal counsel at the National Security Council, to express his concern about what both the president and McClellan had said.

George Tenet followed up Rizzo's call with a memo to Condoleezza Rice, requesting reaffirmation that the CIA's program still had administration approval because "recent Administration responses to inquiries and resulting media reporting about the Administration's position have created the impression that these [interrogation] techniques are not used by US personnel and are no longer approved as a policy matter." Rice held a meeting to discuss the matter in her office on July 29, 2003. Attendees included Muller, Tenet, Gonzales, Cheney, Ashcroft, Bellinger, and Patrick Philbin, acting assistant attorney general from the Office of Legal Counsel. At the meeting, Muller passed out a set of "briefing slides" (presumably print-outs of a PowerPoint presentation) describing the CIA's interrogation program, to be sure that all present would understand what they were approving. Tenet once again expressed displeasure that the White House was telling the press that detainees were being treated "humanely," and Bellinger "undertook to insure [sic] that the White House press office ceases to make statements on the subject other than [to say] that the US is complying with its obligations under US law."

A detailed discussion of waterboarding followed. Tenet then stated that he needed to know that the CIA's interrogation program was not only legal, but that the CIA "was executing Administration policy." Cheney, Rice, and Gonzales all assured him that this was the case. Whatever the CIA was doing, they told Tenet, it had the fully-informed support of the White House, the vice president's office, the Justice Department, and the National Security Council.

Neither Colin Powell nor Donald Rumsfeld was invited to the July 29 meeting in Rice's office. Earlier that month John Rizzo had sent an email to an unknown CIA recipient in which, according to the Senate Committee report, he wrote that "'it is clear to us from some of the runup meetings we had with [White House] Counsel that the [White House] is extremely concerned [Secretary of State] Powell would blow his stack if he were to be briefed on what's been going on." But leaving Powell and Rumsfeld out of the loop made Rice nervous, so she arranged a formal briefing for them on CIA treatment of prisoners, which took place on September 16, 2003.

Nor was this the end of the CIA's search for reassurance. Three years later John Rizzo, who by then was senior deputy general legal counsel for the CIA, asked Steven Bradbury, principal deputy attorney general, very similar questions about the use of "enhanced interrogation techniques," including waterboarding. Bradbury gave Rizzo the answer he was hoping for, in a memo dated May 10, 2005. "In sum," Bradbury wrote, " . . . none of these specific techniques, considered individually, would violate the prohibitions in Sections 2340-2340A."

It is clear from the written record that Vice President Dick Cheney and his office knew and fully approved what the CIA was doing to its prisoners. It is less clear how strongly these methods were endorsed by President Bush. The 2014 Senate Intelligence Committee report on torture stated that "CIA records indicate that the first CIA briefing for the president on the CIA's enhanced interrogation techniques occurred on April 8, 2006," almost five years after John Rizzo received the first two Yoo–Bybee memos at the CIA. The report added, "CIA records state that when the president was briefed, he expressed discomfort with the 'image of a detainee, chained to the ceiling, clothed in a diaper, and forced to go to the bathroom on himself.'"

Nevertheless, Bush did approve the methods when he learned about them and continued to approve them through the end of his presidency. In September 2006, in a televised address, Bush acknowledged the existence of secret CIA "black sites," calling them "a vital tool in the war on terror." Bush strongly defended the CIA, insisting that the agency "treated detainees humanely and did not use torture."

Furthermore, he said, all terror suspects were "afforded protection under the Geneva Conventions." Bush went on to say that the CIA interrogation program was "now complete." But none of this was true.

Almost two years after Bush received his CIA torture briefing, he vetoed the Intelligence Authorization Act for Fiscal Year 2008, which would have required the agency to limit itself to interrogation methods permitted in the US Army Field Manual. He justified his veto by saying the bill "would take away one of the most valuable tools in the war on terror—the CIA program to detain and question key terrorist leaders and operatives."

Afghanistan Nightmare

Kandahar: The results of the CIA's free license to torture during the Bush presidency can be seen in the horrific accounts that have emerged from black sites and other detention centers around the globe, including in Afghanistan. Soon after the start of the war there, the prisoners began piling up. Many were taken to a US airbase in Kandahar, often with untreated wounds. When a plane full of prisoners arrived, the human cargo would be tossed out and onto the ground. Andy Worthington described the routine in *The Guantánamo Files*: "MPs with rubber gloves made them lie on their stomachs while they cut off their clothes." Convinced they were about to be raped, the men "howled and wailed and struggled to turn over." In the next stage of the intake process, prisoners were marched through a tunnel to a holding area, where they received "a quick intelligence screening" and then were pinned to the ground by two MPs, for what they were told in Arabic was "the ass inspection." A doctor would then conduct an anal probe.

Worthington's chapter on Kandahar is worth reading in its entirety to get a sense of the complete abandon that MPs, Special Forces and CIA operatives exercised in their treatment of detainees. Prisoners were indeed raped, and made to watch others being raped. Wounds, including one in which a piece of shrapnel protruded from a man's leg, went untreated. Men like Juma al-Dossari were forced to walk barefoot across barbed wire on the way to "interrogations" and had their faces pushed into broken glass. "Three brothers were blinded" this way, al-Dossari told Worthington.

For the most part, the beatings and torture went on outside the interrogation room. Oddly, the interrogations themselves were usually conducted in accordance with the procedures outlined in the US Military Field Manual, perhaps because the military interrogators had different instructions than the regular guards. There were many exceptions, however. Al-Dossari describes brutal interrogations, including one in which interrogators poured a boiling liquid on his head and put out cigarettes on his foot and wrist. On another occasion, interrogators forced petrol up al-Dossari's anus.

Other prisoners describe similar treatment at Kandahar, along with what would become the familiar litany of sleep deprivation, stress positions, and lengthy exposure to extreme cold, often while soaking wet, in addition to the use of sexual humiliation, death threats, and electric shocks. For many of them, life actually improved once they were sent to Guantánamo.

Turf wars: It is difficult to sort out precisely which US authorities were responsible for these war crimes in the early days in Afghanistan. It seems that most of the abuse came at the hands of regular soldiers and MPs, but it is clear that US Special Forces personnel ran some of the interrogations. The CIA and the FBI were also interrogating at Kandahar, which led to squabbles over "ownership" of the prisoners. Military personnel began to complain that if a prisoner started to produce "interesting information," he'd be whisked off to a CIA detention site at Kabul.

It is clear, however, that the abuse and torture at Kandahar happened under the authority of both Donald Rumsfeld at the Defense Department and George Tenet at the CIA. Their security personnel's freedom to torture was affirmed in Bush's memo of February 2002, in which he reproduced Cheney's and Addington's opinion that no one captured by US forces in Afghanistan was protected by the Geneva Conventions.

The turf war over prisoners between the CIA and the Defense Department continued throughout the Bush presidency. Jeremy Scahill reports in *Dirty Wars* that Rumsfeld and Stephen Cambone, who held a variety of high positions at the Defense Department, "developed a parallel rendition and detention program to the CIA black sites." This Special Access Program bore a number of names—"Copper Green" and "Matchbox" among them. In a *New Yorker* article called "The Gray Zone," reporter Seymour Hersh quoted a highly placed informant, who told him, "We're not going to read more people than necessary into our heart of darkness. The rules are 'Grab whom you must. Do what you want.'" Lieutenant Colonel Anthony Shaffer told Hersh that in Afghanistan the Copper Green cells "had holding points for a prisoner's arms and legs. They were designed for prisoners to be shackled and held in stress positions to maximize discomfort and pain." Shaffer said he had been authorized to use these "highly coercive interrogation techniques" by "my boss at the time, Secretary of Defense Donald Rumsfeld, as well as Stephen Cambone, undersecretary of defense for intelligence."

As part of Copper Green, the Joint Special Operations Command ran its own interrogation operations at a number of military bases in Afghanistan. While the rules of engagement for the NATO coalition directing the war (under US command) set a ninety-six-hour limit on how long a prisoner could be detained, JSOC found ways of holding prisoners for as long as nine weeks, Scahill wrote, while also hiding them from the International Red Cross. JSOC also had its own separate prison for so-called "HVTs" (high-value targets) inside the larger detention facility at Bagram, known as the "Black Jail." JSOC would go on to expand Copper Green in Iraq, where they operated their own prisons, including the one they called Camp Nama.

Bagram and beyond: The CIA also operated several secret black sites in Afghanistan. As early as December 2002, stories about what went on in them began to surface. Dana Priest and Barton Gellman wrote one of the first, for the *Washington Post*. They described a set of shipping containers at Bagram that held "the most valuable prizes in the war on terrorism—captured al Qaeda operatives and Taliban commanders." These prisoners were routinely tormented with "stress and duress" techniques—being shackled in painful positions—along with sensory deprivation, sleep deprivation, and twenty-four-hour bombardment with bright lights. One of the US officials in charge of captured terror suspects interviewed by the *Washington Post* reporters explained his rough methods this way: "If you don't violate someone's human rights some of the time, you probably aren't doing your job." According to this official, the CIA at first had its hands tied by humanitarian concerns. But with the support of the top echelons of the Bush administration, the agency's hands were soon freed.

Once free to go to the dark side, CIA officials began trumpeting their "interrogation successes." On December 11, 2002, George Tenet accepted the Nixon Center's Distinguished Service Award. He used the occasion to remark that Richard Nixon would have approved of the US response to 9/11. CIA interrogations—and those conducted by allies such as Egypt and Saudi Arabia, to whom the CIA had sent prisoners—had been very fruitful, Tenet claimed. But not all of the countries in the anti-terror coalition, hinted the CIA director, were comfortable with what the CIA was doing. "Even the closest of allies differ over tactics and strategy," Tenet said. But sometimes, the US just had to go it alone, without international approval. "With the safety of our country in the balance, there are times when dialogue and engagement are not enough. In intelligence, as in other fields of national security, the principle that guides our actions is a bit less elegant, but no less practical: with others if possible, alone if necessary."

Cofer Black, then head of the CIA Counterterrorist Center, was even more blunt in justifying the agency's methods. Testifying before a joint meeting of the House and Senate Intelligence Committees in September 2002, Cofer stated, "This is a very highly classified area, but I have to say that all you need to know [is]: There was a before 9/11, and there was an after 9/11. After 9/11 the gloves come off."

In addition to the prisons at Bagram and Kandahar, the CIA operated at least one other prison in Afghanistan, known to the agency as the "Salt Pit" and to detainees as the "Dark Prison." Called "site COBALT" in the Senate Intelligence Committee report on CIA interrogations, the Salt Pit was an abandoned brick factory. Over half the 119 CIA prisoners named in the Senate report spent some time at the Salt Pit. Some had been picked up in the Afghanistan theater of war and should therefore have fallen under the protection of one or more of the Geneva Conventions. Others were held there while being transferred from the country where they had been captured to some other destination—Guantánamo, or a third country such as Egypt, Syria, or Morocco. While in the Salt Pit, they lived naked, isolated, and freezing in twenty-four-hour darkness, except when they were paraded around nude for added humiliation.

The Senate Committee report identified Ridha al-Najjar as the Salt Pit's first prisoner. Tenet personally approved his "interrogation" plan, which included bombardment with loud noise, hooding, and sleep deprivation. The report continued:

> More than a month later, on September 21, 2002, CIA interrogators described al-Najjar as "clearly a broken man" and "on the verge of complete breakdown" as result of the isolation. . . .

> In addition, al-Najjar was described as having been left hanging—which involved handcuffing one or both wrists to an overhead bar which would not allow him to lower his arms—for 22 hours each day for two consecutive days, in order to "'break' his resistance." It was also noted al-Najjar was wearing a diaper and had no access to toilet facilities.

"According to the CIA inspector general," the Senate report grimly concluded, "the detention and interrogation of Ridha al-Najjar 'became the model' for handling other CIA detainees at Detention Site Cobalt."

In addition to leaving some prisoners handcuffed in a standing position for as long seventeen days, it appears that interrogators were extraordinarily interested in their prisoners' anuses. It was at the Salt Pit that Khalid Sheikh Mohammed was first introduced to "rectal rehydration." Another prisoner, Mustafa al-Hawsawi, "was later diagnosed with chronic hemorrhoids, an anal fissure, and symptomatic rectal prolapse," according to the Senate report. Nevertheless, in the days following the report's release in December 2014, former Vice President Cheney insisted to NBC's *Meet the Press* that these procedures were done "for medical reasons."

Another important CIA official deeply involved with the Salt Pit was Michael D'Andrea. His name did not become public until April 2015, when *New York Times* reporters Mark Mazzetti and Matt Apuzzo identified "Mr. D'Andrea [as] a senior official in the Counterterrorism Center when the [CIA] opened the Salt Pit.... His counterterrorism officers oversaw the interrogation and waterboarding of Abu Zubaydah, Abd al-Rahim al-Nashiri and Khalid Shaikh Mohammed." Later, D'Andrea became head of the Counterterrorism Center where he "became an architect of the targeted killing program," under which the United States uses drone aircraft to assassinate suspected al Qaeda operatives in several countries.

We know of at least one death at the Salt Pit. In November 2002, Gul Rahman died there, after being subjected to "48 hours of sleep deprivation, auditory overload, total darkness, isolation, a cold shower, and rough treatment," according to the Senate Intelligence Committee report. Rahman was an Afghan citizen who was visiting an old friend, physician Ghairat Baheer, when he was swept up in a raid on Baheer's home in Islamabad, Pakistan. According to a 2010 story in the *Huffington Post,* Baheer is the son-in-law of an Afghan warlord who was believed to be allied with al Qaeda. According to the "US official familiar with the case" who spoke to the *Huffington Post* reporters, Baheer was "a leader of Hezb-e-Islami, an insurgent faction blamed for numerous bombings and violence in Afghanistan." Rahman himself is only referred to in both the *Post* story and the Senate Committee report as "a suspected militant."

The Torture Psychologists: While interrogating Gul Rahman, the CIA called in Bruce Jessen—one of two psychologists who had been consulting with the agency on its handling of prisoners. Jessen and his partner James Mitchell had already directed and participated in the torture of another prisoner, Abu Zubaydah. At the Salt Pit, it was Jessen who planned the forty-eight hours of torment for Rahman, although he had left the facility by the time Rahman was found shackled to the wall, half naked and dead of exposure in his 36-degree cell. The Senate Committee report notes that "Prior to [Jessen's] departure from the detention site [in] November 2002, [Jessen] proposed the use of the CIA's enhanced interrogation techniques on other detainees and offered suggestions to . . . the site manager, on the use of such techniques."

John Bruce Jessen and James Elmer Mitchell had each been instructors at the Air Force's SERE (Survival, Evasion, Resistance, and Escape) school, where elite soldiers were taught to withstand, as the Senate report put it, "the conditions and treatment to which they might be subjected if taken prisoner by countries that do not adhere to the Geneva Conventions." In 2002, Jessen and Mitchell were called in to CIA headquarters for discussions about possible methods for interrogating war on terror prisoners—presumably methods that did "not adhere to the Geneva Conventions." Jessen and Mitchell drew up the first list of techniques to be used on detainee Abu Zubaydah. (See Chapter 5.) The suggested methods included confinement in small spaces, waterboarding, and "walling"—slamming the back of a detainee's head against the wall, which according to CIA guidelines was permissible to do "twenty or thirty times consecutively . . . if the interrogator requires a more significant response to a question." All of these methods were approved by Jay Bybee at the Justice Department's Office of Legal Counsel in his August 2002 memo for CIA counsel John Rizzo.

The CIA hired Jessen and Mitchell as contractors to design and oversee interrogations. In 2005, the two psychologists formed a private company, which eventually earned $81 million in consulting fees from the agency. The CIA's contract with Jessen and Mitchell's company was terminated in 2009, but the agency has continued to pay their legal bills through a separate "indemnification" agreement. According to the Senate Committee report, "Under the CIA's indemnification contract, the CIA is obligated to pay [the company's] legal expenses through 2021."

Jessen and Mitchell adapted the "interrogation" methods they sold to the CIA from the work of Martin Seligman, a well-respected American psychologist, who had done research on what he called "learned helplessness." Why did the CIA need to hire outsiders to teach them interrogation? The Senate Intelligence Committee asked the agency that question, too. Here's the CIA's reply, found in a footnote of the committee report. ("SWIGERT" and "DUNBAR" are the Committee's pseudonyms for Mitchell and Jessen, respectively.)

"Drs. [SWIGERT] and [DUNBAR] had the closest proximate expertise CIA sought at the beginning of the program, specifically in the area of *non-standard means of interrogation*. Experts on traditional interrogation methods did not meet this requirement. Non-standard interrogation methodologies were not an area of expertise of CIA officers or of the US Government generally. We believe their expertise was so unique that we would have been derelict had we *not* sought them out when it became clear that CIA would be heading into the uncharted territory of the program (emphasis in original).

The Senate report emphasized that Jessen and Mitchell bear substantial responsibility for the CIA's adoption of these specific methods of torture. The "CIA did not seek out SWIGERT and DUNBAR after a decision was made to use coercive interrogation techniques," stated the report, "rather, SWIGERT and DUNBAR played a role in convincing the CIA to adopt such a policy."

Oddly enough, the two psychologists may have been simply repackaging the extreme interrogation research that the CIA itself had sponsored during the Cold War—and of course selling it back to the agency for millions of dollars. Under the massive "brain warfare" research program authorized by CIA director Allen Dulles in 1953—code-named MKULTRA—the agency had recruited an army of elite researchers and institutions to develop ways of breaking down prisoners. Unfortunate human guinea pigs—including captured Soviet agents, prison convicts and mental patients—were subjected to a variety of brutal "brainwashing" techniques (including overdoses of experimental drugs) that sometimes resulted in death. The objective was to set the conditions for successful questioning by creating a psychological "regression" to infancy in a prisoner. The results of this research, summarized in a 1963 manual called *KUBARK Counterintelligence Interrogation*, include recommendations for the use of techniques that are now familiar to the world: truth serums, sensory deprivation, sensory bombardment, sleep deprivation, and painful stress positions.

The CIA manual was reissued in 1983 as the *Human Resource Exploitation Training Manual,* which was used to interrogate prisoners during President Reagan's war against the Sandinista government in Nicaragua, and in other hot zones of the Cold War. A redacted but highly readable version was declassified in 1997. It seems likely that Jessen and Mitchell were among the manual's more devoted readers.

War Crimes in Iraq

Abu Ghraib: On a Wednesday evening in April 2004, the CBS news show *Sixty Minutes II* shocked the nation when it broadcast a series of photographs from a prison in Iraq called Abu Ghraib. In image after image, grinning US soldiers stacked naked prisoners like cordwood, posed them shackled and hooded in humiliating and stressful positions, and led one nude captive like a dog with a collar and leash. The story of Abu Ghraib had, through the work of reporter Seymour Hersh, finally reached the public eye. (Later, *Salon. com* would publish a larger gallery of photos, some of them even more disturbing, along with nineteen short videos. One of these depicted a man attempting to kill himself by banging his head repeatedly against a steel door.)

Situated about twenty miles outside Baghdad, the prison at Abu Ghraib was well known to Iraqis. Under Saddam Hussein, it had held thousands of prisoners and had a fearsome reputation for torture. In 2003, the US military needed a place to house detainees, and Abu Ghraib (although not perhaps the best choice for winning Iraqi hearts and minds) was ready-made for the purpose. Thousands of detainees were imprisoned there, many of them in tents on the grounds, where they were vulnerable to not-infrequent mortar attacks. For those taken inside however, things were worse, as the pictures demonstrated.

Once the images of Abu Ghraib began their global journey, the US government had a problem. Apart from occasional references to the need to work "the dark side," the Bush administration had been telling the world that US treatment of its prisoners was "humane." That was not what the world saw in those photographs. It was time for damage control. The Joint Chiefs chairman Richard B. Myers, Defense Secretary Donald Rumsfeld, and President Bush himself spoke to the press, in an attempt to reduce the sickening impact of the photos.

Their unanimous message was that these terrible pictures represented the unfortunate aberrations of a few poorly trained reservists. "There was sadism on the night shift at Abu Ghraib, sadism that was certainly not authorized," said James Schlesinger, the old Washington hand who chaired a four-member panel Rumsfeld assigned to investigate. In the view of Rumsfeld's panel, the beatings, threatened electrocutions, rape, anal penetration with foreign objects (including, according to Major General Antonio Taguba's report on Abu Ghraib, "with a chemical light and perhaps a broom stick"), enforced standing, sleep deprivation, dog attacks, and other torture were the work of an isolated handful of depraved individuals. These low-ranking service members, with no outside instigation and for no particular reason, had invented a series of vicious and highly effective methods of torture and humiliation to use on the people in their care. The truth, of course, was very different.

CNN reported in 2004 that Schlesinger had found "no policy of abuse" operating at Abu Ghraib. On the contrary, "Senior officials repeatedly said that in Iraq, Geneva regulations would apply." Senior officials may have "said" as much to Schlesinger and his fellow panelists, but as we have seen, there was in fact a "policy of abuse" that had already been put in place by the CIA for their work in Afghanistan. The Office of Legal Counsel had already issued its memos to the CIA defining "torture" as pain consistent with "organ failure or even death," and approving a list of methods that would later come to be called enhanced interrogation techniques. It was not simply a case of "grab-ass" behavior getting out of control in the lower ranks, as one Military Police officer told the *Washington Post*. What happened at Abu Ghraib was the logical result of official policy developed at the highest level of the Bush administration.

The CIA and Military Intelligence were in charge of the interrogations at Abu Ghraib. Members of the 800th Military Police Brigade, many of them reservists who worked as prison guards in civilian life, were responsible for guarding the Abu Ghraib detainees whom the CIA planned to interrogate. The MPs were told that their job was to "set the conditions" for interrogation by brutalizing their charges. If they did a good job, they were allowed to watch the "OGA" (Other Government Agency, i.e., the CIA) operatives and their private contractor assistants do the real dirty work. One reservist, Staff Sergeant Ivan Frederick II, was almost pathetically eager to please. An email home reads in part:

> It is very interresting [sic] to watch them interrogate these people. They don't usually allow others to watch them interrogate but since they like the way I run the prison they make an exception. . . .

We have had a very high rate with our style of getting them to break. They usually end up breaking within hours.

Before the public revelations of torture at Abu Ghraib, the Pentagon had already deployed Major General Antonio Taguba to investigate. He wrote a searing report, which was leaked to the press, after which he was forced into early retirement for his trouble. The Taguba Report spread the blame for the Abu Ghraib outrages widely. In addition to CIA and Military Intelligence interrogators, Taguba made it clear that private contractors were also guilty of torturing prisoners at Abu Ghraib. Taguba mentioned two in particular, both employees of the Virginia- and London-based CACI Corporation, working for the 205th Military Intelligence Brigade.

Although he had access to many of the personnel at Abu Ghraib, Taguba faced one important constraint: military protocol decreed that he was not permitted to investigate the complicity of anyone of his own rank or higher. So his report, devastating as it was, is silent on the role played by his superiors at the Pentagon, including General Geoffrey Miller (to whom we will return) and, of course, head of the Joint Chiefs, Richard B. Myers, or Rumsfeld himself.

Nonetheless, Taguba's report frustrated the administration's attempt to pin all the blame on reservists engaging in "sadism on the night shift." Abu Ghraib revealed the very essence of the Bush administration's treatment of those swept up in the war on terror.

No one above the rank of sergeant was ever prosecuted for any of the abuse at Abu Ghraib, including the two known deaths. In one case, the CIA tortured Manadel al-Jamadi to death by cuffing his hands behind his back and then hanging him by his wrists from the bars of a window until he died. Al-Jamadi was a "ghost prisoner." He'd never been officially registered, and his presence at Abu Ghraib was hidden from the International Red Cross. He may not have existed officially, but his body did, and now the CIA had another problem: how to get rid of the corpse? Staff Sergeant Frederick wrote home about this as well:

> They put his body in a body bag and packed him in ice for approximately 24 hours in the shower in the 1B. The next day the medics came in and put his body on a stretcher, placed a fake IV in his arm and took him away. This OGA [prisoner in the hands of an Other Government Agency—the CIA] was never processed and therefore never had a number.

Medical examiners ruled al-Jamadi's death while he was in the hands of CIA interrogators a homicide. Years later, Eric Holder, who served as President Obama's attorney general from 2009 to 2015, promised an investigation, but no one was ever prosecuted.

What were the interrogators at Abu Ghraib hoping to discover by subjecting their captives to such treatment? Even assuming that torture is an effective (or legal) tool for intelligence gathering—an idea that has been repeatedly debunked by many experts—the treatment inflicted on prisoners at Abu Ghraib seems inexplicable. If it was battlefield intelligence that the CIA was seeking, the interrogations were useless because they often took place months after prisoners were first detained and most information related to the safety of US soldiers would have been long outdated. If not battlefield information, what were the CIA and its private contractors looking for?

One hint comes from something Joint Chiefs chairman Richard Myers told the NBC *Today* show in May 2003, a few months into the Iraq war. None of the administration's vaunted weapons of mass destruction had turned up in Iraq, and the main pretext for the invasion was crumbling. "Given time, *given the number of prisoners now that we're interrogating* [emphasis added], I'm confident that we're going to find weapons of mass destruction," said General Myers. Apparently at least part of the Bush administration felt the truth about WMDs could be wrung out of its Iraqi captives.

The Confessions of "Osama bin Laden"

Saddam Saleh Aboud spoke to *New York Times* reporter Ian Fisher in May 2004, shortly after the story of Abu Ghraib first broke in the United States. Aboud was a Sunni businessman with an unfortunate first name who'd gone to an Iraqi police station to report a suspected car bomb. Instead of thanking him, the Iraqi police turned him over to the US military, and he found himself in Block 1-A of Abu Ghraib, the section where Charles Graner, Lynndie England, and their cohorts "softened up" prisoners for interrogation.

Aboud was tortured for almost three weeks at Abu Ghraib. He was blindfolded and forced to stand on a box with his arms outstretched. He was struck with a broomstick, first on his hands, then on his arms, his shoulders and his stomach. When he fell off the box, his tormenters threw cold water on him. One of them urinated on him. The next day he was taken to see a sergeant who told him,

"If you do not confess, I will have my soldiers rape you."
The threat was not an empty one. Aboud does not say
that he was raped, but Maj. General Anthony Taguba's
catalog of outrages at Abu Ghraib includes such practices as "[s]odomizing a detainee with a chemical light
and perhaps a broom stick." The report also mentions
a "male MP guard having sex with a female detainee."
Under the circumstances at Abu Ghraib, an American
soldier "having sex with" an Iraqi woman detainee can
only be a euphemism for "raping."

Saddam Aboud spent most of his eighteen days
at Abu Ghraib chained twenty-three hours a day in
a sitting position with his arms over his head while
unbearably loud music played. "Every few days,"
according to the *New York Times*, "he was uncuffed
for other treatments: douses of cold water, barking
dogs, something called 'the scorpion,' in which his
arms were cuffed to his legs, behind his back " while
he was kicked and beaten. Finally, it was time for the
questions.

"They began talking to me," Aboud told the *Times*.
"They asked, 'Do you know the Islamic opposition?' I
said, 'Yes.' They asked, 'Do you know Zarqawi?'" referring to Abu Musab al-
Zarqawi, a Jordanian militant with ties to Al Qaeda.
"I told them, 'I am his driver, I swear to God.'"
Having (falsely) confessed to being the driver for a
man the US considered an elite terrorist, Aboud then
made an even more startling admission. "They asked

me about Osama bin Laden. I said, 'I am Osama bin Laden but I am disguised.'" Aboud said he meant every word. "I was only afraid that they would take me back to the torture room. I would prefer to be dead."

But, of course, no prisoners could reveal the whereabouts of Saddam's secret nuclear, chemical and biological weapons factories because they didn't exist.

Who is responsible for what happened at Abu Ghraib? There is plenty of blame to go around, but much of it falls on the shoulders of Donald Rumsfeld, whose wishes were carried out by his deputy Stephen Cambone, and further down the chain of command, by Major General Geoffrey Miller.

In November 2002, Miller was placed in charge of interrogations at Guantánamo. Under pressure from Rumsfeld to produce more useful intelligence, Miller sought approval to use more coercive methods on his prisoners. (By "useful intelligence," Rumsfeld and other top Bush officials probably meant evidence of a Saddam-9/11 connection—a connection as illusory as Saddam's WMD factories.) In December 2002, Jim Haynes, the Defense Department's general counsel, sent a memo to Rumsfeld recommending approval of a number of coercive techniques, including stress positions, isolation, sleep deprivation, and exploiting prisoners' personal phobias, such as fear of dogs. The memo indicates that both Douglas Feith and Richard Myers concurred. So did Rumsfeld—but he added a handwritten note suggesting that forcing a prisoner to stand for a few hours was not particularly stressful. "I stand for 8–10 hours a day. Why is standing limited to 4 hours?" he wrote.

In September 2003, Rumsfeld dispatched Maj. General Miller to Iraq, to oversee detentions there, especially Abu Ghraib. His mission? To "Gitmo-ize" the place. In April 2004, Miller formally took charge of all US detentions and interrogations in Iraq. Miller quickly introduced the aggressive new procedures he brought from Guantánamo, including one he especially favored—the use of military dogs to frighten detainees. Apparently, the new procedures produced results that were more like what the Pentagon wanted—although the "intelligence" gathered this way often proved to be a mix of invention and desperate agreement to whatever interrogators suggested. Miller had indeed succeeded in Gitmo-izing Iraq.

In a July 28, 2005, story, the *Washington Post* reported on a little-noticed preliminary hearing for two Army dog-handlers, who were facing court martial for their use of dogs to torment prisoners at Abu Ghraib. Testimony at this hearing underlined Miller's role in bringing Guantánamo's methods to Iraq. Major David DiNenna, identified by the *Post* as "the top military police operations officer at Abu Ghraib in 2003," told the court, "We understood [Miller] was sent over by the secretary of defense, to take their interrogation techniques they used at Guantánamo Bay and incorporate them into Iraq." The *Post* story continued:

While methods employed at Abu Ghraib—including hooding, nudity and placing prisoners in stress positions—have been characterized by senior defense officials as rogue, abusive horseplay on the night shift, some of them had been authorized for experienced interrogators at Guantanamo Bay. Dogs, seen menacing detainees at Abu Ghraib in grisly photographs, were also used in Cuba under Miller's command.

One of the dog handlers, Sgt. Michael J. Smith, was convicted of various charges in 2006, including using dogs to terrify prisoners into urinating and defecating on themselves. Colonel Thomas M. Papas, who had been in charge of military intelligence at Abu Ghraib during the period captured on the photographs, testified for the defense—under a grant of immunity. He testified that he had learned about the "effectiveness" of military dogs from Miller and his entourage, when they first visited Iraq in 2003. Miller was called to testify

A Hero at Abu Ghraib

If it hadn't been for a twenty-four-year-old soldier named Joe Darby, we might never have heard of the tortures and abuses committed at Abu Ghraib. Darby was a member of a Military Police unit assigned to the prison. One day early in 2004, Army Specialist Charles Graner handed him a couple of CDs full of photographs, thinking perhaps that Darby would enjoy them as much as he did. Graner was one of the people in charge of the Army Reservists responsible for "softening up" prisoners before they were handed over for interrogation to Military Intelligence and the "Other Government Agency" (a euphemism for the CIA and its private contractors).

When Joe Darby saw the photographs, unlike Graner he was not amused. He was horrified. He recognized the revolting images as evidence of crimes and, after three weeks of interior debate, he decided to hand them to Special Agent Tyler Pieron of the US

Army Criminal Investigation Command, who was working at Abu Ghraib. From there, the photos made their way up the chain of command, and finally—via a leak to reporter Seymour Hersh—into US living rooms on *60 Minutes II*.

Darby hoped to remain anonymous, but he soon gained international renown for what he had done. With exposure came threats to him and to his family. In the immediate aftermath of the disclosures, while still stationed at Abu Ghraib, he feared that he might be murdered in his sleep. Still, he doesn't consider what he did anything special. As he said when accepting the Kennedy Library's Profiles in Courage award, "It just seemed like the right thing to do at the time."

for the defense at the trials for both dog handlers. He refused, citing his Fifth Amendment right not to incriminate himself.

Camp Nama: Abu Ghraib is infamous, but war crimes were also committed at JSOC's Camp Nama, located near the Baghdad airport. Nama was not its real name. Officially, it was the Battle Field Interrogation Facility. Nama stood for "Nasty-Assed Military Area," according to a 2006 Eric Schmitt story in the *New York Times*. Its motto, which could be seen on posters in the facility, was "No blood, no foul," an allusion to the belief that "If you don't make them bleed, they can't prosecute you for it." Detainees at Camp Nama were considered not to be prisoners of war, and therefore outside the protection of the Geneva Conventions. They were permitted no visitors—not family members, lawyers, or representatives of the International Red Cross.

Journalist Jeremy Scahill reported on the treatment of one Camp Nama prisoner, the son of a Saddam Hussein bodyguard. He said that he "was made to strip, was punched repeatedly in the spine until he fainted, was doused with cold water and forced to stand in front of the air-conditioner and kicked in the stomach until he vomited."

This was a typical ordeal for those prisoners who fell into JSOC's hands. These unfortunate Iraqis were beaten, sodomized, exposed to relentless noise and light, drenched with cold water, and made to stand dripping for hours in front of air conditioners. Some died. Many had no information to offer because they didn't know anything their interrogators wanted to hear. In fact, a leaked Red Cross report from the period quotes US military intelligence officers as saying "that in their estimate between 70% and 90% of the persons deprived of their liberty in Iraq had been arrested by mistake."

So secret was Camp Nama that when Maj. General Miller was on his "Gitmo-izing" tour of Iraq, he needed special permission from the very top of the Pentagon to gain admittance. Who *did* know what went on in the detention centers run by JSOC in Iraq? First, there was General Stanley McChrystal, who commanded JSOC from September 2003 through 2008. He was a frequent visitor at Camp Nama and fully aware of all that went on there. According to a 2009 *Esquire* magazine interview with an interrogator who worked at Nama, McChrystal guaranteed that no one could interfere with the interrogation procedures at Nama. The colonel in charge of the prison told the interrogator that he "had it directly from General McChrystal and the Pentagon that there's no way that the Red Cross could get in—they won't have access and they never will. This facility was completely closed off to anybody investigating, even Army investigators."

McChrystal's military duties during the Bush administration extended far beyond Camp Nama. Under his direction, JSOC became the force that Dick Cheney and Donald
Rumsfeld used to run a full-bore covert operations network.
(See Chapter 5.) There may have been another reason Cheney
and Rumsfeld preferred to run their special ops out of the
Pentagon, rather than through the CIA. As Mark Mazzetti
wrote in a 2010 *New York Times* article, "Unlike covert
actions undertaken by the CIA, such clandestine activity
does not require the president's approval or regular reports
to Congress."

Responsibility for war crimes at Camp Nama extends
beyond McChrystal to Rumsfeld and to Cheney, and ultimately, to commander in chief George W. Bush, although
it is unclear how much he actually knew about the JSOC's
activities.

In 2009, President Obama appointed McChrystal to head
US and coalition forces in Afghanistan. The commander fell
afoul of Obama the following year, when he made dismis-
sive remarks about the president to *Rolling Stone* reporter
Michael Hastings. McChrystal was forced to resign, but
neither his forced departure from the military nor the leg-
acy of Camp Nama and JSOC's other horrors cast a shadow
over the retired general. After his retirement, he was given
a lucrative book contract, was asked to teach a course on
leadership at Yale, and has remained an influential voice in
military circles.

General David Petraeus: In 2004, General David Petraeus
became head of the Multi-National Security Transition
Command in Iraq. For Petraeus, it was another high-level
posting in the midst of a dynamic career that would later place
him in charge of US and coalition forces in Afghanistan and

then, briefly, would give him command of President Obama's CIA (until he was felled by scandal). As head of the multi-national command in Iraq, part of the general's job involved training the Iraqi Special Police Commandos, an elite group whose remit included interrogation of prisoners suspected of participating in the insurgency against the new, US-installed government. Rumsfeld sent Petraeus a colonel named James Steele to help with this project. Steele had a lot of experience with interrogation procedures, including torture. During Reagan's wars in Central America, he had been one of the key advisors to the repressive right-wing governments in El Salvador, overseeing many activities at Ilopango Air Force Base, site of a well-known torture center.

Petraeus recruited retired Colonel James H. Coffman to help Steele set up the detention centers and train interrogators in Iraq. Coffman reported directly to Petraeus, and Steele to Rumsfeld. The *Guardian* later interviewed Iraqi general Muntadher al-Samari, who assisted Coffman and Steele. "They worked hand in hand," Samari told the *Guardian's* reporters. "I never saw them apart in the 40 or 50 times I saw them inside the detention centers. They knew everything that was going on there . . . the torture, the most horrible kinds of torture." Samari went on to detail the interrogation procedures employed by the detention facilities overseen by Coffman and Steele:

> Every single detention centre would have its own interrogation committee . . . . Each one was made up of an intelligence officer and eight interrogators. This committee will use all means of torture to make the detainee confess like using electricity or hanging him upside down, pulling out their nails, and beating them on sensitive parts.

Was teaching Iraqi Special Police Commandos torture methods a war crime? It very likely was. In any case, it was certainly a violation of the US federal code, which makes torture committed "outside the United States" a punishable offense.

Most of the war crimes described here are violations both of the international laws and customs of war, including the Geneva Conventions, and of the 1996 US War Crimes Act. The CIA under George Tenet suspected that this might be the case, which is why the agency repeatedly sought reassurance from the Office of Legal Counsel. It is why in 2002 the United States withdrew from the treaty creating the International Criminal Court. Perhaps the ICC cannot try these officials and private contractors for war crimes, but the US federal courts still have jurisdiction over violations of Section 2340 of the federal code (the federal anti-torture law) and the War Crimes Act.

Fallujah: An American Atrocity The US military assaults on Fallujah, a center of anti-American resistance during the Iraq War, were ferocious. The civilian population was subjected to intensive bombardment by the US Air Force that, according to some sources, involved cluster bombs. Many residents of the city were caught in withering crossfire, while others were cut down by sniper fire. By 2004, the city was largely reduced to rubble, with sixty percent of its buildings destroyed, and most of the city's three hundred thousand people displaced or killed. The havoc of war continues to haunt the people of Fallujah, who suffer from unusually high rates of cancers and birth defects.

One of the uglier aspects of the US military's battle for Fallujah was the use of white phosphorus, an incendiary munition. Phosphorus ignites spontaneously when it is exposed to air. When bits of the chemical attach to human beings, the skin and flesh burn away. The burning continues as long as there is oxygen available to combine with the phosphorus, sometimes continuing right down to the bone.

In November 2005, the Associated Press ran a story about a documentary produced by a state-run Italian news channel, which alleged that the United States had used white phosphorus in a "massive and indiscriminate way" against civilians during the Fallujah offensive. The US government issued contradictory responses, with the State Department initially acknowledging that phosphorus had been used, but only to "provide illumination," and later retracting this statement. Meanwhile, a Pentagon spokesperson confirmed that white phosphorus had in fact been used "as an incendiary weapon against enemy combatants" but not against civilians.

Whether civilians or enemy fighters are the targets, the use of white phosphorus is almost certainly a war crime as defined in the 1996 War Crimes Act. The federal law prohibits "grave breaches" of the 1907 Hague Convention, and this appears to be just such a breach. Article 23(e) of the Hague charter makes it unlawful to "employ arms, projectiles, or material calculated to cause unnecessary suffering." The use of incendiary weapons of any kind, including white phosphorus, is explicitly prohibited in Protocol III of the UN Convention on Certain Conventional Weapons. Unfortunately, the United States has not signed Protocol III.

It is perhaps particularly ironic that the United States should invade Iraq on the grounds that Saddam Hussein was producing and stockpiling chemical weapons, only to employ its own chemical weapons against Iraqis.

In the next chapter, we will turn to another category of crimes—those committed outside the wars in Iraq and Afghanistan and which therefore may not directly contravene the laws and customs of war, but which violate equally important international agreements protecting human rights.

Table of Principal US Officials, Private Security Corporations, and Civilians Who Could Be Charged With War Crimes, Related to the Wars in Afghanistan and Iraq

Name	Position
David Addington	Minority Counsel to the House-Senate Committee investigating Iran-Contra: 1987 Chief Counsel to US Vice-President: 2001–2005 Chief of Staff to US Vice President: November 1, 2005–January 20, 2009
Michael D'Andrea	Chief of Operations and Director, CIA Counterterrorism Center: 2001-2015
John Ashcroft	US Attorney General: February 2, 2001–February 3, 2005
Cofer Black	Director of the CIA's Counterterrorist Center: June 1999–2002 US State Department Ambassador at Large and Coordinator for Counterterrorism: 2002–November 2004 Vice Chairman of Blackwater USA: 2005–2008
Steven Bradbury	Principal Deputy Assistant Attorney General for Office of Legal Counsel of the Department of Justice: April 2004 Acting Assistant Attorney General for Office of Legal Counsel (never confirmed by Senate), 2005–2009
George W. Bush	US President: January 20, 2001–January 20, 2009
Jay Bybee	Assistant Attorney General, Office of Legal Counsel of the Department of Justice: January 2001–March 13, 2003
CACI International Inc.	Contractor furnishing interrogators to US detention facility at Abu Ghraib: 2004

Name	Position
Stephen Cambone	Under Secretary of Defense for Intelligence: March 7, 2003–December 31, 2006
Col. James Coffman	US Army: advisor along with Steele to Iraqi death squad, "Wolf Brigade": 2004
Dick Cheney	Vice President: January 20, 2001–January 20, 2009
Lieutenant Gen. Dell L. Dailey	Commander of Joint Special Operations Command: 2001–2003 US State Department Coordinator for Counterterrorism: June 22, 2007–April 2009
Douglas Feith	Under Secretary of Defense for Policy (G.W. Bush/Rumsfeld): July 2001–August 2005
Alberto Gonzales	White House Counsel: January 20, 2001–February 3, 2005 United States Attorney General: February 3, 2005–September 17, 2007
William J. "Jim" Haynes	General Counsel of the Department of Defense: May 24, 2001–March 10, 2008
John "Bruce" Jessen	US Air Force psychologist leading the Survival, Evasion, Resistance and Escape (SERE) training: before 1988 Principal in Mitchell, Jessen & Associates, contractors to the CIA for interrogation: 2002–April 2009
Gen. Stanley McChrystal	Commander, Joint Special Operations Command: 2003–2008 Commander, International Security Assistance Force (ISAF) and Commander, US Forces Afghanistan (USFOR-A): June 15, 2009–June 23, 2010
Major Gen. Geoffrey Miller	Commander of US detention facilities at Guantánamo Bay, Cuba and in Iraq: November 2002–November 2004

Name	Position
James Elmer Mitchell	US Air Force psychologist leading the Survival, Evasion, Resistance and Escape (SERE) training for part of service: 1988–2001 Principal in Mitchell, Jessen & Associates, contractors to the CIA for interrogation: 2002–April 2009
Scott Muller	General Counsel of the CIA: 2002–2004
Gen. Richard Myers	Chairman of the Joint Chiefs of Staff (G.W. Bush): October 1, 2001–September 30, 2005
Gen. David Petraeus	Commander, Multi-National Force—Iraq: February 10, 2007–September 16, 2008 Commander US Central Command: October 31, 2008–June 23, 2010 Commander US and ISAF forces in Afghanistan: July 4, 2010–July 18, 2011 Director of the US CIA: September 6, 2011–November 9, 2012
Condaleezza Rice	US National Security Advisor (G.W. Bush): January 20, 2001–January 26, 2005 US Secretary of State (G.W. Bush): January 26, 2005–January 20, 2009
John Rizzo	Acting General Counsel of the CIA: November 2001–2002; Deputy General Counsel: 2002–2004; Acting General Counsel of the CIA: again mid-2004–October 2009
Donald Rumsfeld	US Secretary of Defense (G.W. Bush): January 20, 2001–December 18, 2006
Col. James Steele	US "military advisor": Vietnam, El Salvador (1984 to 1986), US occupation of Iraq (2004)
George Tenet	Director of Central Intelligence (Clinton & G W Bush): December 15, 1996–July 11, 2004
John Yoo	Deputy Assistant Attorney General, Office of Legal Counsel, US Department of Justice: 2001–2003

Chapter 5

Crimes Against Human Rights

We don't kick the shit out of them. We send them to other countries so they can kick the shit out of them.

—Anonymous US official speaking to reporters in 2002

If you are going to murder someone, you need to have a very good reason to do it, and you need to have absolutely unequivocal evidence that this is necessary, and will materially advance our interests. And that just doesn't happen.

—Joshua Foust, former Yemen analyst for the
Defense Intelligence Agency

This chapter describes actions in the war on terror—actions such as torture, enforced disappearance, and assassinations—that would be war crimes if they were committed in the context of an actual war. When the United States mistreated any prisoner in either Iraq or Afghanistan, regardless of the person's combatant status, this mistreatment was a violation of the Geneva Conventions as well as the US War Crimes Act, and for both these reasons was a war crime. However, such crimes fall into a different category when committed in a conflict that has no defined geographical boundaries or foreseeable endpoint; a war fought in fits and starts in many countries on several continents; a war carried on through covert operations and, to the extent possible, hidden from everyone except its targets. Such a war lacks the regular, sustained conflict between armies that characterizes war in the legal sense. Thus, the crimes committed in this never-ending war on terror, outside of the Afghanistan and Iraq theaters of combat, are not really war crimes. But they are still terrible crimes, even when they occur outside the confines of a traditional war.

Torture, for example, always violates the UN Convention against Torture, and is clearly illegal under international law. Because the United States has signed and ratified the convention, torture is always illegal under US domestic law as well. Furthermore, when the United States tortures someone outside US territory, then as we saw in Chapter 2, a specific US law comes into play—section §2340 of the US criminal code—which outlaws torture outside the United States.

When the CIA kidnapped Abd al-Rahim al-Nashiri in Dubai, transported him to a dark site in Poland, strung him up by the wrists for sixty hours and put a pistol and an electric drill to his head, the agency broke quite a few human rights laws and treaties. However, while Nashiri's kidnapping and torture are terrible crimes, it is not at all clear that—absent an actual war—they can be called war crimes. That is why I've chosen to collect crimes like this in a category called "human rights crimes."

US human rights crimes in the war on terror include such actions as kidnapping and enforced disappearance; torture; rendition (sending a prisoner to another country to be tortured); hostage taking and detention without trial; human experimentation; and extrajudicial killing. All of these are illegal under one or more international human rights conventions, and many are illegal under US laws, too.

As is the case with the war crimes described in the previous chapter, US officials at the highest levels are responsible for these human rights crimes. These include George W. Bush, Dick Cheney, Donald Rumsfeld, and their coterie of top deputies and lawyers, as well as high-ranking members of the Obama administration, including President Barack Obama himself, who has personally approved extrajudicial assassinations carried out by the remotely piloted aircraft known as drones.

Kidnapping, Rendition, and Torture

We will probably never know how many people were kidnapped in countries such as Pakistan, Indonesia, or Macedonia and shipped to secret CIA prisons under the Bush administration. We will never know how many were sent from CIA prisons to be tortured in other countries. The latter procedure is called "extraordinary rendition," and it did not originate with George W. Bush. The history of such political kidnapping (with or without rendition) extends at least as far back as the Cold War, but it accelerated under President Bill Clinton.

Clinton knew it was illegal. In his 2004 memoir *Against All Enemies: Inside America's War on Terror*, counter-terrorism chief Richard E. Clarke describes an Oval Office meeting in 1993. Clarke had proposed to "snatch" an (unnamed) terrorist, and Clinton's White House Legal Counsel Lloyd Cutler was explaining why this would violate international law. Al Gore came in late to the meeting and got a summary of the arguments on both sides from Clinton. Clarke, with obvious approval, reproduced Gore's take on the question: "That's a no brainer. Of course it's a violation of international law, that's why it's a covert action. The guy is a terrorist. Go grab his ass."

According to Clarke, during the Clinton administration, the impediment to successful snatches wasn't to be found in the White House. It was George Tenet's CIA that couldn't—or wouldn't—carry them out. The Department of Defense was no better at devising kidnapping operations; in one case, observed Clarke, the Pentagon brass could only "generate options" that would have led to a ground war in Sudan. The only force that seemed to have the right stuff in Clarke's view was the Joint Special Operations Command, but this gung ho unit was often stymied by "senior military." That would change under George W. Bush.

The "snatches" Clarke describes were primarily kidnappings, rather than renditions. Several of the people arrested this way were brought to the United States and tried in civilian courts for participating in the 1993 World Trade Center bombing. True rendition means transferring someone from one legal jurisdiction to another, usually through legal extradition. Rendition becomes "extraordinary" when it happens outside the law, as when a person is sent to a country with which the United States does not have an extradition treaty, and/or when it is likely (or certain) that the rendered person will be tortured in that other country.

In a 2004 *New Yorker* magazine article and later in her book, *The Dark Side*, Jane Mayer described a secret agreement between Egypt and the United States that was forged under President Clinton. The US would seize the targets—some of whom were already wanted in Egypt—and render them to that country. Technically, the Clinton administration was required to secure written assurance from Egypt that the rendered persons would not be tortured. But, as former CIA agent Michael Scheuer told a congressional hearing, such assurances "weren't worth a bucket of warm spit." The rendition targets were tortured, and some were executed.

Ordinarily, when one country wishes to bring criminal charges against someone in another country, the prosecuting country uses the legal method of extradition. It presents evidence showing probable cause to the government of the country where the subject is living, and that country makes a decision whether or not to extradite. The CIA had a problem with ordinary extradition, however, because the agency really had no evidence against many of the people it wanted to imprison. Indeed, sometimes the "evidence" only emerged after the target was interrogated under torture. Other times, it was information produced by torturing one person that led the CIA to snatch someone else. And of course, as is so often the case with tortured testimony, the information was often wrong. In any case, the United States didn't want to put its targets on trial in a public venue, which is the usual goal of extradition. So they resorted to kidnapping.

What was extraordinary rendition like under George W. Bush? First, it was a surprisingly large program, expanding greatly from the Clinton years. In a 2013 report, "Globalizing Torture: CIA Secret Detention and Extraordinary Rendition," the Open Society Foundation listed fifty-four countries involved in the US rendition program. And it was brutal. Evidence of this can be found in important books such as *The Guantánamo Files* by Andy Worthington, who collected the stories of 774 Guantánamo detainees. *Guantánamo*

Diary by former Gitmo prisoner Mohamedou Ould Slahi is also an extraordinary document. In an English-language record given to his US attorneys, Slahi used his fourth or fifth language not only to tell his own story, but to give us very human sketches of the many—and varied—people responsible for his torments (and occasional joys) after his detention in November 2001.

With one exception, no US officials have been prosecuted for any of these kidnappings. The exception is a case brought by Italy against twenty-six US citizens, most of them CIA operatives, for the kidnap and rendition to Egypt of Hassan Mustafa Osama Nasr. Twenty-three of those charged—including Robert Seldon Lady, the then-CIA station chief in Milan, and US Air Force Lieutenant Colonel Joseph L. Romano—were convicted in absentia in 2009. The United States, notwithstanding its 1983 extradition treaty with Italy, has refused to turn over the convicted Americans.

What happened to Hassan Nasr? He was snatched off the streets of Milan in February 2003 and transported to Egypt, where, according to a 2008 *Washington Post* story, "he was tortured for months with electric shocks and shackled to an iron rack known as 'the Bride.'" His torturers threw him onto a wet mattress, and while one sat in a wooden chair pinning his shoulders down, "another interrogator would flip a switch, sending jolts of electricity into the mattress coils," forcing the electric current through his immobilized body.

At the time of his kidnapping, Nasr was in exile from Egypt and living in Italy, where he had found political asylum. He was serving as an imam at an Islamic institute in Milan. There he apparently preached frequent sermons against US policies in Afghanistan and the Middle East, and may have been trying to recruit fighters for the Afghanistan War. It is not clear why the CIA, which was working with the

Italian Military Intelligence and Security Service, suddenly decided to kidnap Nasr, particularly since the agency had tapped his phone and was developing intelligence from his conversations with potential jihadis. The Italian newspaper *La Repubblica* suggested Nasr's kidnapping was an attempt to provide the "slam dunk" evidence of an al Qaeda–Saddam Hussein link, which George Tenet had promised to give Dick Cheney and George W. Bush. Nasr's experience, reported the Italian newspaper, was just a "chapter in the . . . intelligence–psychological warfare–information war engaged in by Washington and London to justify the invasion of Iraq."

Nasr's rendition to Egypt violated Article 3 of the UN Convention against Torture, which reads, "No State Party shall expel, return ("refouler") or extradite a person to another State where there are substantial grounds for believing that he would be in danger of being subjected to torture." Similarly, the US Foreign Affairs Reform and Restructuring Act of 1998 holds that

> it shall be the policy of the United States not to expel, extradite, or otherwise effect the involuntary return of any person to a country in which there are substantial grounds for believing the person would be in danger of being subjected to torture, regardless of whether the person is physically present in the United States.

Perhaps the CIA didn't get the memo. In any case, the agency seems to have developed its own rendition criteria. Former CIA agent Robert Baer explained the methodology to British *New Statesman* reporter Stephen Grey: "If you want a serious interrogation, you send a prisoner to Jordan. If you want them to be tortured, you send them to Syria. If you want someone to disappear—never to see them again—you send them to

Egypt." Or, as an unnamed US official told *Washington Post* reporters Dana Priest and Barton Gellen in 2002, "We don't kick the shit out of them. We send them to other countries so they can kick the shit out of them."

The Case of Binyam Mohammed

Binyam Mohammed was a young man in his early twenties who held asylum rights in England. He was arrested while visiting Pakistan and turned over to the Americans, who—as I've written elsewhere—decided he was connected to the so-called "dirty bomber" José Padilla. The Americans sent him from Pakistan to Morocco, because "the Pakistanis can't do exactly what we want them to."

Mohammed's testimony about what happened next appears in Andrew Worthington's *The Guantánamo Files*. His Moroccan jailers cut his clothes off with a scalpel, which they then turned on his chest. Then, "one of them took my penis in his hand and began to make cuts. He did it once, and then they stood still for maybe a minute, watching my reaction. I was in agony." They didn't stop. "They must have done this twenty to thirty times in maybe two hours. There was blood all over." This happened once a month for eighteen months, after which Mohammed was happy to tell the interrogators anything they wanted to hear.

"About once a week or even once every two weeks," Mohammed told Worthington, "I would be taken for interrogation, where they would tell me what to say. They said if you say this story as we read it, you will just go to court as a witness and all this torture will stop." So that's what Mohammed did. "Eventually," he says, he "repeated what was read out to me." Among those he implicated were "big people" Mohammed had never heard of before the torture—José Padilla, Khalid Sheikh Mohammed, Abu Zubaydah and Ibn al-Shaykh al-Libi.

Torture and Detention Without Trial: In fact, the CIA was also doing its own kicking. From 2001 until at least 2009, the agency ran secret prisons in several countries besides the ones in the combat theaters of Afghanistan and Iraq. Countries that have been identified include Cuba (at Guantánamo), Lithuania, Poland, Romania, and Thailand, as well as the British island territory of Diego Garcia in the Indian Ocean.

Although President Obama ordered all the agency's black sites closed when he took office in 2009, the CIA continues to run at least one interrogation center. It is located in Mogadishu, Somalia, where, according to a December 2014 report by Jeremy Scahill in the *Nation* magazine, CIA agents are training Somalia's National Security Agency in interrogation methods. Scahill reported that US agents "also directly interrogate" suspected militants of the al Shebab network. According to former detainees, the underground prison "consists of a long corridor lined with filthy small cells infested with bedbugs and mosquitoes" where prisoners pace their cells or sit rocking endlessly back and forth. Some have not seen daylight in more than a year.

On August 1, 2002, Jay Bybee, assistant attorney general in the Bush Justice Department, sent a memo to John Rizzo, then acting general counsel at the CIA, addressing

Rizzo's questions about what the agency could do to a prisoner named Abu Zubaydah without running afoul of US anti-torture law. Zubaydah, a so-called "high-value detainee" and supposedly a top aide of Osama bin Laden, had just been captured in Pakistan and was being held at "Detention Site Green," the CIA's black site in Thailand. Bybee's memo assured Rizzo that waterboarding Zubaydah, among other sorts of "proposed conduct" that Rizzo had suggested, would not violate US laws prohibiting torture.

Bybee's memo reminded Rizzo that the CIA had described Abu Zubaydah as "one of the highest ranking members of the al Qaeda terrorist organization." Furthermore,

> according to [the CIA] assessment, Zubaydah, though only 31, rose quickly from very low level mujahedin to third or fourth man in al Qaeda. He has served as Usama Bin Laden's senior lieutenant. In that capacity, he has managed a network of training camps. He has been instrumental in the training of operatives for al Qaeda, the Egyptian Islamic Jihad, and other terrorist elements inside Pakistan and Afghanistan . . . . He also acted as al Qaeda's coordinator of external contacts and foreign communications.

None of this was actually true, as documents from Zubaydah's *habeas corpus* hearings eventually revealed. Who, then, is Abu Zubaydah? He is a Saudi national presently imprisoned in Guantánamo. In the 1980s he does seem to have held a responsible position at Khalden Camp in Afghanistan, a mujahideen training camp established with CIA help during the Soviet occupation. In effect, Zubaydah was a US ally in the fight against the Soviets in Afghanistan.

For several years, the Bush administration routinely referred to Khalden as an al Qaeda training camp, but in fact, it was not. The Senate Intelligence Committee report made this clear when it quoted a CIA Intelligence Assessment dated August 16, 2006, entitled "Countering Misconceptions About Training Camps in Afghanistan, 1990–2001." The CIA assessment observed that "a common misperception in outside articles is that Khaldan camp was run by al-Qa'ida." This "misconception" developed, according to the CIA document, because the agency's pre-9/11 intelligence had inaccurately cast Zubaydah as "a senior al-Qa'ida lieutenant." The CIA knew this was wrong, and knew, in fact, that Zubaydah was not even connected to al Qaeda.

Nevertheless, the month after the CIA clarified the nature of the Khalden camp and Zubaydah's lack of al-Qaeda connections, President Bush used the story of Zubaydah's capture and interrogation to publicly justify the CIA's "enhanced interrogation" program, telling the public that, "he helped smuggle Al Qaida leaders out of Afghanistan." The administration's reasoning about Zubaydah's role seems to have run in a perfect circle: Zubaydah ran Khalden; therefore Khalden was an al Qaeda camp. Khalden was an al Qaeda camp, therefore Zubaydah was a senior al Qaeda official.

In August 2002, Pakistani forces captured Zubaydah. In the process, he was severely injured, with bullet wounds in the thigh, testicle, and stomach. He would have died, had the CIA not imported a US surgeon to patch him up. The CIA's interest in Zubaydah's health was far from humanitarian, however. The agency wanted to interrogate him. In fact, after he had recovered sufficiently to be questioned, his captors occasionally withheld pain medication as a means of torture.

Abu Zubaydah was the first human subject on whom CIA-funded psychologists Bruce Jessen and James Mitchell had the opportunity to test their theories about using torture to induce "learned helplessness." CIA records show that interrogators used the waterboard on Zubaydah eighty-three times. During this ordeal, the Senate committee reported, he became "completely unresponsive, with bubbles rising through his open, full mouth." Each "iteration of the watering cycle" consisted of four steps:

1) demands for information interspersed with the application of the water just short of blocking his airway 2) escalation of the amount of water applied until it blocked his airway and he started to have involuntary spasms 3) raising the water-board to clear subject's airway 4) lowering of the water-board and return to demands for information.

The CIA videotaped these "watering cycles," but in 2005, then-CIA Director Michael Hayden ordered the tapes destroyed. In addition to waterboarding, Zubaydah endured the usual sleep deprivation, exposure to loud noises, "walling" and confinement for hours in a box so small he could not stand up inside it.

It was also with Zubaydah that the CIA began its practice of hiding detainees from the International Committee of the Red Cross by transferring them to its dark sites. The Senate Intelligence Committee report corroborated this. "In part to avoid declaring Abu Zubaydah to the International Committee of the Red Cross, which would be required if he were detained at a US military base," stated the report, "the CIA decided to seek authorization to clandestinely detain Abu Zubaydah at a facility in Country _____ [now known to have been Thailand]."

Hayden would later tell the press that 25 percent of all the information that the CIA had gathered about al Qaeda from human sources "originated" with Abu Zubaydah. Even if this were true, this "information" must have been of dubious value, since Zubaydah was not a member of al-Qaeda. Zubaydah had nothing to do with the "Millennium" plots to attack US targets in Jordan and Los Angeles in 2000, as had been alleged. There was no Saddam-al Qaeda link, although Zubaydah's "testimony" was used to establish one. Zubaydah was not, as Bush once described him to guests at the Connecticut Republican Committee Luncheon at the White House, "one of the top operatives plotting and planning death and destruction on the United States." He had nothing to do with the bombing of the USS *Cole*, in spite of what Bush told the nation at the end of 2001. By the time of his September 2006 speech, Bush had inflated the allegations against Zubaydah to include logistical support for the 9/11 attacks themselves. In a speech justifying "enhanced interrogation techniques," Bush told the nation, "Our intelligence community believes [Abu Zubaydah] had run a terrorist camp in Afghanistan where some of the 9/11 hijackers trained."

In June 2007, the Bush administration doubled down on its claim that Zubaydah was involved with 9/11. At a hearing before the congressional Commission on Security and Cooperation in Europe, State Department Legal Adviser John Bellinger was explaining to the commission on behalf of then Secretary of State Condoleezza Rice why the Guantánamo prison needed to remain open. Guantánamo, said Bellinger, "serves a very important purpose, to hold and detain individuals who are extremely dangerous," like "Abu Zubaydah, people who have been planners of 9/11." Nor was Zubaydah, as Donald Rumsfeld said on numerous occasions, "a very senior al Qaeda official who has been intimately involved in a range of activities for the al Qaeda" or "if not the number two, very close to the number two person in the organization."

The United States quietly withdrew all these allegations against Abu Zubaydah in September 2009. Zubaydah's attorneys had filed a *habeas corpus* petition on his behalf, and in that context were asking the government to supply certain documents to help substantiate their claim that his continued detention in Guantánamo was illegal. The Obama administration replied to this request with a 109-page brief filed in the US District Court in the District of Columbia—the court that is legally designated to hear Guantánamo detainees' *habeas* cases. Buried in the middle of this brief lay the government's argument that there was no reason to turn over any "exculpatory" documents that would demonstrate that Zubaydah was not a member of al Qaeda, or that he had no involvement in 9/11 or any other terrorist activity—*because the government was no longer claiming that any of those things were true.*

The government's lawyers went on to make the stunning declaration that the Bush administration had *never* "contended that [Zubaydah] had any personal involvement in planning or executing either the 1998 embassy bombings in Nairobi, Kenya, and Dar-es-Salaam, Tanzania, or the attacks of September 11, 2001." Furthermore, "the Government also has not contended in this proceeding that at the time of his capture, [Zubaydah] had knowledge of any specific impending terrorist operations." This is particularly telling, given that it was the prevention of future attacks that justified the CIA's torture of Zubaydah in the first place. The brief went on to argue that, far from believing that he was "if not the number two, very close to the number two person in" al Qaeda as Rumsfeld had said, "the Government has not contended in this proceeding that [Zubaydah] was a member of al-Qaida or otherwise formally identified with al-Qaida."

Nevertheless, in his 2010 memoir, *Decision Points*, George W. Bush continued to maintain the fiction that Zubaydah had been such a threat to the United States that the nation could only be protected if he were tortured:

> Had I not authorized waterboarding on senior al Qaeda leaders, I would have had to accept a greater risk that the country would be attacked. In the wake of 9/11, that was a risk I was unwilling to take. My most solemn responsibility as president was to protect the country. I approved the use of the interrogation techniques.

Since, as far as we have been told, only two people were subjected to waterboarding—Khalid Sheikh Mohammed and Abu Zubayda, one of those "senior al Qaeda leaders" Bush refers to must be Zubaydah.

Seven years after the initial filing of Zubaydah's *habeas* petition, the DC District Court has yet to rule on it. This is an extraordinary length of time, compared to the court's average 751-day turnaround time. Here, justice delayed is truly justice denied. Perhaps we should not be surprised, however. According to the Senate Intelligence Committee report, CIA headquarters assured those who were interrogating Zubaydah that he would "never be placed in a situation where he has any significant contact with others and/or has the opportunity to be released." In fact, "All major players are in concurrence," stated the agency, that he "should remain incommunicado for the remainder of his life."

Abu Zubaydah is not the only US prisoner in the war on terror who has never been charged with any crime, either in civilian courts or a military tribunal. The Obama administration has continued the practice of indefinite detention without trial begun under the 2001 congressional Authorization for the Use of Military Force against al Qaeda. In a signing statement appended to the 2011 National Defense Authorization Act, President Obama reiterated the United States' right to hold non-US citizens indefinitely. On the other hand, he rejected the view that all prisoners seized as potential terrorists must be handed over to the military. Obama has repeatedly argued that many such people can and should be tried in civilian courts.

Nonetheless, as of this writing, fifty-one men who have been cleared for release from Guantánamo—some cleared years ago—are still being held there. Most of these are Yemenis. It seems unlikely they will be able to return home anytime soon, even if the United States were prepared to release them. Yemen is presently locked in a vicious civil war in which Saudi Arabia, the central US ally in the region, has intervened, with the assistance of US money and munitions. Almost sixty other Gitmo detainees have neither been cleared for release nor charged with any offense. They remain in the same legal limbo they entered when they were first imprisoned in the top-security island compound more than a dozen years ago. Many of them are held in continual solitary confinement, itself widely recognized as a form of torture. If and when they are eventually released, they will have lost many years of their lives to illegal detention without charge or trial.

Those who resist their detention through the only non-violent tactic available to them—the hunger strike—are also tortured with punitive force feedings. Yemeni detainee Samir Naji al Hasan Moqbel described the procedure in a 2013 guest column in the *New York Times*:

I will never forget the first time they passed the feeding tube up my nose. I can't describe how painful it is to be force-fed this way. As it was thrust in, it made me feel like throwing up. I wanted to vomit, but I couldn't. There was agony in my chest, throat and stomach. I had never experienced such pain before. I would not wish this cruel punishment upon anyone.

I am still being force-fed. Two times a day they tie me to a chair in my cell. My arms, legs and head are strapped down. I never know when they will come. Sometimes they come during the night, as late as 11 p.m., when I'm sleeping.

As of late 2015, Moqbel was still incarcerated at Guantánamo.

A few other men remain at Guantánamo—such as Abu Zubaydah and Khalid Sheikh Mohammed—whom the US government deems "too dangerous" ever to release but who can never be tried because the "evidence" against them was produced under torture. Some of them are named and their tortures described in the Senate Intelligence Committee report.

Finally, we know almost nothing about who is being held in secret sites like the one that the CIA operates jointly with Somali forces, or that JSOC may well be operating in any of the "fifty to sixty countries" where Defense Secretary Rumsfeld told CBS News in 2001 that al Qaeda and other "networks of terrorists" are active.

Human Experimentation

The 1996 US War Crimes Act lists "[pe]rforming biological experiments" as one of the "grave breaches" of Geneva constituting a war crime. A biological experiment is defined as any "act of a person who subjects, or conspires or attempts to subject, one or more persons within his custody or physical control to biological experiments without a legitimate medical or dental purpose and in so doing endangers the body or health of such person or persons." Certainly the United States has not conducted the number or kind of experiments in the course of the war on terror that the Nazi doctors carried out at Auschwitz and other concentration camps. Thousands of people died and thousands more were tortured, maimed, and mutilated in the service of Nazi pseudo science. At a 1946 trial held at Nuremberg, the United States prosecuted twenty Nazi doctors, of whom thirteen were convicted of war crimes and crimes against humanity. US experimentation took place on a much smaller scale during the war on terror, but it did happen.

Almost every regime that introduces the practice of torture keeps careful records of its work. This was true of the Nazis in the 1930s and '40s, as well as of the military dictatorship in Brazil, which ruled from 1964 to 1985.

The CIA was no exception during the years following 9/11. In a May 30, 2005, memo from Steven Bradbury, head of the Justice Department's Office of Legal Counsel, to John Rizzo, then acting general counsel at the CIA, Bradbury discussed the CIA's record-keeping. Rizzo had written once again to secure reassurance that "enhanced interrogation techniques" are "consistent with the United States obligations under Article 16" of the UN Convention against Torture, which forbids "cruel, inhuman or degrading treatment or punishment which do not amount to torture." In his reply, Bradbury explained that there was method to the CIA's brutality.

"Careful records are kept of each interrogation," Bradbury wrote. This procedure, he continued, "ensures accountability and allows for *ongoing evaluation of the efficacy of each technique* [emphasis added] and its potential for any unintended or inappropriate results." In other words, the CIA kept careful records of what was at least in part an experimental procedure designed to observe how well waterboarding worked. This was Abu Zubaydah's impression as well. "I was told during this period that I was one of the first to receive these interrogation techniques," Zubaydah told the International Committee of the Red Cross, "so no rules applied. It felt like they were experimenting and trying out techniques to be used later on other people."

In addition to videotaping the use of the waterboard, the CIA's Office of Medical Services required a meticulous written record of every waterboarding session. The details that were to be recorded are spelled out clearly:

> In order to best inform future medical judgments and recommendations, it is important that every application of the waterboard be thoroughly documented: how long each application (and the entire procedure) lasted, how much water was used in the process (realizing that much splashes off), how exactly the water was applied, if a seal was achieved, if the naso- or oropharynx was filled, what sort of volume was expelled, how long was the break between applications, and how the subject looked between each treatment.

It is possible to interpret this requirement of thorough documentation as evidence of the CIA's concern for the welfare of their detainees. Another reading is equally possible however: these are the records of an experimental procedure. The details about amount of water used; whether or not a "seal" was achieved (so no air could enter the victim's lungs); whether the naso- or oropharynx was filled (in other words, whether the nose and throat were so full of water the victim could not breathe); how much the "subject" vomited up; and how he "looked between each treatment"—all of these become additional data points in ongoing research into "effective" techniques of interrogation.

The medical veneer glossing this inhumane experimentation makes it all the more appalling. It was the two psychologists Jessen and Mitchell who brought waterboarding to the CIA. They personally used the torture method on detainees and taught others how to do it. It is not unreasonable to suppose that they helped design the protocols for data collection as well.

This was not the first time that the CIA has engaged in human experimentation. As we saw in Chapter 4, the CIA's Cold War research program codenamed MKULTRA paid hundreds of elite researchers and institutions to experiment on involuntary human subjects, using psychedelic drugs, isolation regimens and other "brainwashing" techniques in an effort to control people's minds. Indeed, as a result of the 1975 Church Commission hearings into CIA abuses, President Gerald Ford issued an executive order prohibiting the CIA from engaging in "experimentation with drugs on human subjects"—a prohibition later expanded in executive orders issued by Presidents Carter and Reagan to include any kind of nonconsensual experimentation on human beings. Carter's Executive Order 12333 stated clearly in Section 2.10, "No agency within the Intelligence Community shall sponsor, contract for or conduct research on human subjects except in accordance with guidelines issued by the Department of Health and Human Services. The subject's informed consent shall be documented as required by those guidelines."

But this executive order on human experimentation was flagrantly violated during the war on terror. It seems that psychological consultants like Jessen and Mitchell were hired specifically to engage in this sort of "research."

In fact, a 2004 CIA document from the agency's own Inspector General's office—the department that is supposed to ensure legal and ethical conduct in the agency—suggests that the IG wanted the CIA to engage in more research on enhanced interrogation techniques (EITs). The IG observed that "[i]nasmuch as EITs have been used only since August 2002, and they have not all been used with every high value detainee, there is limited data on which to assess their individual effectiveness." If only the CIA had tortured more people, the data would have been more complete. This is relevant, the IG review continued, because "[d]etermining the effectiveness of each EIT is important in facilitating Agency management's decision as to which techniques should be used and for how long." Better data, better "effectiveness." Entirely apart from the fact that the Senate Intelligence Committee report thoroughly refuted CIA claims of effectiveness, testing different methods of torture to see "which techniques should be used and for how long" is human experimentation and—under Geneva and US law—a war crime.

The IG review went on to identify specific difficulties encountered by anyone trying to make rigorous study of various torture methods: "Measuring the overall effectiveness of EITs is challenging for a number of reasons, including: (1) the Agency cannot determine with any certainty the totality of the intelligence the detainee actually possesses." In other words, there's no way to measure "effectiveness" in this experiment, because you can never really know what the subject knows (if anything). So how can you decide whether he's told you everything he knows? Torture him. In fact, CIA cable traffic referred to in the Senate report suggests that interrogators of Abu Zubaydah took exactly this approach.

They were no longer using torture to encourage Zubaydah to give up information about threats to US safety, but rather "to achieve a high degree of confidence that [Abu Zubaydah] is not holding back actionable information concerning" such threats.

There were other challenges to successful measurement of "the overall effectiveness" of CIA interrogation methods, such as the fact that "(2) each detainee has different fears of and tolerance for EIT." So it was difficult to know whether to attribute the "success" of an interrogation method to the strength of the technique or the weakness of the detainee. Furthermore, it was difficult to standardize the experimental procedures because "(3) the application of the same EITs by different interrogators may have different results." A fourth difficulty is left to our imaginations; it is redacted in the Inspector General's review. Although they never called it "research," it is clear that the CIA was engaged in a semi-formal program of experimentation on human subjects, complete with objectives (to measure "the overall effectiveness of EITs") and a protocol for careful documentation of each procedure. These are human rights crimes.

Assassination and Extrajudicial Killing

When President Barack Obama took office, looking for a way to continue the war on terror while avoiding US casualties, he turned to the remote-controlled aerial drone program. Under Obama, the use of drones expanded nine-fold over the drone strikes of the Bush era, with growing numbers of attacks on human targets in Pakistan, Yemen, and Somalia, as well as in the Afghanistan and Iraq war zones. As the deadly bolts from the sky struck villages, farm fields and roads, and the "collateral" civilian casualties mounted, anti-drone outrage spread throughout the regions where they were used. And many, even within US national security circles, began to question the efficacy of the escalating drone war, wondering whether the strikes were creating more enemies in the region than they were eliminating.

As a result, in May 2013, President Obama publicly announced a shift in his drone strategy, telling an audience at the National Defense University that the United States would engage in "targeted killings" of al Qaeda militants only when there was a "near-certainty" that no civilians would be injured. He added that he was planning to make the US drone program more transparent than it had been, and to transfer most of its operations from the CIA to the Pentagon. None of this has happened. Many civilians continue to be killed by drone strikes, and their homes and property destroyed. Transparency has hardly increased since Obama's speech. The drone program remains swathed in secrecy. And despite Obama's announced intention to transfer responsibility for the program to the Pentagon, the CIA continues to run most of it, with the exception of strikes carried out by the equally secretive Joint Special Operations Command. Finally, even Obama's stated policy of tightly targeting al Qaeda "militants" is a human rights crime. These remote-controlled assassinations are extrajudicial killings—executions that take place outside the rule and processes of the law.

Three months after Obama spoke at the National Defense University, Arafat Qa'id Salem Arfaj and his three brothers, Hussein, Hasan, and Abdullah, went shopping for holiday supplies in the Yemeni city of Marib. In "Death by Drone," a report written for the Open Society Foundation, Armit Singh describes what happened next. The brothers bought food and new clothes for their family in celebration of Eid al Fitr, the end of the Muslim holy fasting month of Ramadan.

Now they were driving home in two cars, Arafat up front, and his younger brothers bringing up the rear in their 1998 red Suzuki Vitara. They'd just called their mother. "Put Eid henna on your hands," they told her. "We are on the way!"

Arafat's three brothers never made it. Moments later a drone fired four missiles, one of which hit the Suzuki and set it on fire. Arafat rushed to the car, where he found his three brothers dead. He told an interviewer what he saw:

> The children's clothes and shoes and the Eid supplies were scattered all around. The body of Abdullah was about 10 meters away from the car. Hussein had turned into a burned body under the car. The body of Hasan was headless and charred, lying about two meters to the right of the car.

Hussein, the youngest brother, was just fifteen years old. None of the three who died that day were HVTs—High Value Targets. None of them were top-level al Qaeda leaders. None of them had anything whatsoever to do with the US-identified enemy in Yemen at the time, al Qaeda in the Arabian Peninsula, or AQAP. They were just four brothers on their way home to celebrate one of the most joyful days in the Muslim calendar.

In February 2013, President Obama nominated John O. Brennan, his assistant for homeland security and counterterrorism, to replace Leon Panetta as CIA director. In his confirmation hearings, senators queried Brennan about the US drone program and civilian deaths. He said such deaths were few and far between. Furthermore, "in those rare instances in which civilians have been killed, after-action reviews have been conducted to identify corrective actions and to minimize the risk of innocents being killed or injured in the future." But the researchers who compiled the Open Society Foundation report on the drone attack on the Arfaj brothers stated there is no evidence of any "after-action review" in the deaths of the Arfaj brothers following the killings—or in any of the eight other US drone attacks discussed in the report, all of which took place in Yemen between 2012 and 2014 and resulted in civilian deaths. Brennan also told the senators that it was US policy to pay financial compensation to families of victims. "Where possible," he said, "we also work with local governments to gather facts and, if appropriate, provide condolence payments to families of those killed." None of the families interviewed for the Open Society report had ever been offered any kind of compensation for the deaths of their family members.

The drone assassination program began under George W. Bush, with a 2002 strike in Yemen, which killed Qaed Salim Sinan al-Harethi and five others, including a US citizen named Kamal Derwish. The Bush administration maintained that al-Harethi was a top al Qaeda operative and the mastermind of the bombing of the USS *Cole* in 2000.

The program grew during the Bush presidency, primarily in Pakistan. Because of the secrecy surrounding drone strikes it is difficult to say how many operations Bush ordered and how many people died as a result. A New America Foundation report based on mainstream news coverage identified forty-eight drone strikes in Pakistan between 2004 and 2008, resulting in the deaths of between 115 and 141 civilians and between 205 and 350 "militants." According to the same report, in Pakistan alone, the Obama administration has ordered 351 strikes, killing between 1,864 and 3,066 civilians and between 1,581 and 2,634 "militants."

In Pakistan, over sixty percent of all strikes target domestic buildings—people's houses—according to the Bureau of

Investigative Journalism. In other words, in addition to killing people, including many civilians, drone strikes frequently destroy the homes of any survivors.

A February 2015 report by the Bureau of Investigative Journalism found that only eleven percent of the victims of drone strikes in Pakistan could be clearly identified as "militants." Little was known about the many other victims.

Except for the one strike that killed al-Harethi, all 129 (as of August 2015) drone attacks in Yemen have occurred under President Obama. The Obama administration's Department of Justice has argued that these drone strikes are not "assassinations" and are legal under the laws of war. In a paper dated November 8, 2011, a little over a month after the 2011 drone attack that killed US citizen Anwar al-Awlaki, the department's Office of Legal Counsel responded to a request (it is not clear from whom) for an opinion on the legality of the use of "lethal force in a foreign country outside the area of active hostilities against a US citizen who is a senior operational leader of al-Qa'ida or an associated force of al-Qa'ida—that is, an al-Qa'ida leader actively engaged in planning operations to kill Americans." In other words, after the fact, someone in the Obama administration wanted to know whether it had been legal to kill Anwar al-Awlaki in a location other than Iraq or Afghanistan, in this case, in Yemen.

The anonymous DOJ author identified four sources of the president's authority to kill such a person: 1) his "constitutional responsibility to protect the country," 2) "the inherent right of the United States to national self defense under international law," 3) "Congress's authorization of the use of all necessary and appropriate military force against this enemy" (referring here to the 2001 Authorization for the Use of Military Force), and 4) "the existence of an armed conflict with al-Qa'ida under international law."

Furthermore, the DOJ paper argued, killing such an individual does not violate President Jimmy Carter's Executive Order 12333, which stated, "No person employed by or acting on behalf of the United States Government shall engage in, or conspire to engage in, assassination." This is because "[a] lawful killing in self-defense is not an assassination . . . . In the Department's view, a lethal operation conducted against a US citizen whose conduct poses an imminent threat of violent attack against the United States would be a legitimate act of national self-defense that would not violate the assassination ban." Finally, the Justice Department paper outlined three requirements for legally killing Al-Awlaki—and presumably, for killing anyone else who fit these criteria:

> (1) an informed, high-level official of the US government has determined that the targeted individual poses an imminent threat of violent attack against the United States; (2) capture is infeasible, and the United States continues to monitor whether capture becomes feasible; and (3) the operation would be conducted in a manner consistent with applicable law of war principles.

As we saw in Chapter 5, international law does indeed grant nations the right of self-defense when attacked, but preemptive self-defense is a trickier question. In the classic *Caroline* case—deriving from a 19th century international incident involving the US, British and Canadian governments—the standard established for legitimate preemption was that the need for "self-defense is instant, overwhelming, and leaving no choice of means, and no moment for deliberation." The Justice Department paper seemed to endorse this view when it required that a high

US official determine that "an imminent threat of violent attack against the United States" exists.

However, the paper went on to explain that "imminent" doesn't really mean "imminent" in the sense that something is about to happen. In fact, "the condition that an operational leader present an 'imminent' threat of violent attack against the United States does not require the United States to have clear evidence that a specific attack on US persons and interests will take place in the immediate future." It turns out that the threat from any "operational leader" is always imminent, because, "with respect to al-Qa'ida leaders who are continually planning attacks, the United States is likely to have only a limited window of opportunity within which to defend Americans." In other words, once a person has been identified as an al Qaeda or allied group "leader," he is by definition "continually planning attacks," and therefore always represents an imminent danger—and a legitimate target.

The UN Special Rapporteur on Extrajudicial, Summary or Arbitrary Executions has disagreed with this view. In his 2013 report to the UN General Assembly, Christof Heyns described the international legal framework in which drone strikes take place: international human rights law, international humanitarian law (the laws of war), and the laws governing conflicts between nations. International human rights law guarantees a right to life, which is enshrined in the 1948 Universal Declaration of Human Rights and given legal force in, among other treaties, the International Covenant on Civil and Political Rights, to which the United States is a party. There are legal limits to the right to life, including—in countries that have the death penalty—the state's right to execute a person after a legitimate trial. To execute someone *without* a trial, however, is an "extrajudicial killing," and it is a human rights crime.

This is why it matters so much whether the conflict between the United States and various terrorist organizations is really a war. If not, then the law that applies is international human rights law (along with domestic laws against murder). If the war on terror is not a war, then the United States had no legal right to kill one of its own citizens, such as Anwar al-Awlaki, without a trial. Indeed, it has no right to kill anyone who is not immediately threatening the lives of Americans. Human rights law does allow killing under very specific circumstances in order to save human lives. As the UN Special Rapporteur stated, "Where intentional killing is the *only* [emphasis added] way to protect against an imminent threat to life, it may be used. This could be the case, for example, during some hostage situations or in response to a truly imminent threat."

The assertion that simply because someone is a "leader," he must by definition be "continually planning attacks"—as the Justice Department paper argued—doesn't justify extrajudicial killing. That is, it doesn't justify such killing unless the low-level conflict that includes drone strikes in Pakistan, Yemen, and Somalia constitutes a true war. In that case, the looser strictures of international humanitarian law (the laws of war) would come into play. In war, the human right to life does not apply to those who are engaged in combat. Civilians still have that right, which is protected by the Geneva Conventions, but combatants become legitimate targets. In that case, it could be argued that drone strikes against identified belligerents are legal, as would be the inevitable deaths of some civilians as "collateral damage."

But, as I have argued, the war on terror is not a war in the legal sense. The UN Special Rapporteur, in agreement with the International Committee of the Red Cross, also takes the position. "For a conflict to qualify as a non-international armed conflict," he says, "armed violence must also reach a certain threshold of intensity that is higher than that of internal disturbances and tensions." And it has to keep going on. "The armed violence should not be sporadic or isolated but protracted." Whatever the US conflict with "terror" may be, it is not a war. And the people who are killed in drone strikes, even if some of them are actually by some definition terrorists, have a right to life under international human rights law. Killing them without due process is murder.

In any case, it appears that President Obama has jettisoned even the Justice Department's limited set of requirements for its drone strikes—at least in Pakistan, where the majority of attacks during his administration have taken place. An April 15, 2015, *Wall Street Journal* story reported that Obama secretly "waived" the requirement that a target represent imminent danger when the CIA plans drone strikes in Pakistan. In practice this means that the CIA does not even identify a specific, named human target, but instead relies on what it calls "signature strikes."

Signature strikes target unidentified individuals based on some "signature" activity, usually activity observed by surveillance drones. The "signature" can be as ill-defined as "a gathering of men, teenaged to middle-aged, traveling in convoys or carrying weapons," according to a 2015 *Guardian* story. A 2012 *New York Times* article reported a joke going around the State Department at the time: "When the C.I.A. sees 'three guys doing jumping jacks,' the agency thinks it is a terrorist training camp."

In countries like Yemen or Pakistan, where most men carry rifles, and many social events involve groups of people driving from one town to another, even a wedding can appear to have the "signature" of terrorism. This is what happened in

Yemen in December 2013, when missiles fired from a drone killed at least twelve people traveling in a wedding party. A survivor, Abdullah Muhammad al-Tisi, described the carnage to Human Rights Watch:

> We were having a traditional marriage ceremony. According to our traditions, the whole tribe has to go to the bride's tribe. We were in about 12 to 15 cars with 60 to 70 men on board. We had lunch at the bride's village at Al Abu Saraimah. Then we left to head back to the groom's village.
>
> A drone was hovering overhead all morning. There were one or two of them. One of the missiles hit the car. The car was totally burned. Four other cars were also struck. When we stopped, we heard the drone fire. Blood was everywhere, and the people killed and injured were scattered everywhere. The area was full of blood, dead bodies and injured people.

One aspect of the mostly secret drone program is not a secret. As has been widely reported, President Obama personally decides who should live or die at a grim ritual held each Tuesday, during which Obama reviews "kill lists" with Pentagon and CIA officials. The US press has often treated this Tuesday meeting with a respect bordering on awe. American citizens are asked to marvel at the awesome power, the high seriousness, the heroic suffering of the lonely man at the top. Lonely, perhaps, but not entirely alone. "Beside the president at every step," wrote Jo Becker and Scott Shane in a 2012 *New York Times* article, "is his counterterrorism adviser, John O. Brennan." According to the *Times* report, colleagues described the Catholic-educated Brennan as "a priest whose blessing has become indispensable to Mr. Obama, echoing the president's attempt to apply the 'just war' theories of Christian philosophers to a brutal modern conflict."

It would seem, however, that the US war on terror violates several of the tenets of just war theory, not least the requirement—also found in international humanitarian and human rights law—of proportionality. A country's actions must be proportional to the harm it has suffered, or the imminent danger it faces. In what sense can we call the deaths of hundreds of thousands of Iraqis and Afghans, thousands of Pakistanis and Yemenis, the millions of people made refugees, proportional to what the United States suffered on 9/11? And according to what moral calculus is it justified to repeatedly blow up civilian families and individuals in the process of trying to assassinate terror suspects? For that matter, why is it proper for the US government to kill even these suspects—people who live outside war zones and may or may not be guilty of belligerent actions—without the due process of law? Certainly, as the case of Abu Zubaydah demonstrates, the government does not have a good record of identifying "al Qaeda leaders."

Just war theory also requires distinguishing between combatants and others, and as much as possible, avoiding doing harm to the latter. The drone war has a terrible record in this regard as well. To take one example, secret documents published by the *Intercept* in October 2015 demonstrated that in twenty-seven attacks in northeastern Afghanistan over a five month period, *almost ninety percent* of those killed were not the targeted individuals. They were simply unfortunate people who happened to be in the vicinity of the attacks.

In the aftermath of the November 2015 terror attacks in Paris, leading politicians in both parties almost fell over themselves in the race to propose sufficiently muscular responses.

Republican presidential candidate Ted Cruz suggested that ISIS could only be fought effectively if the US stopped caring so much about collateral damage. ISIS, said Cruz in a statement posted on his web site, "will not be deterred by targeted airstrikes with zero tolerance for civilian casualties." In other words, we should punish ISIS for killing civilians by—killing civilians.

Of course this disregard for civilian casualties was already an indelible stain on the Obama presidency. So, along with the Bush administration officials guilty of initiating the drone war, we must add the Obama administration officials—beginning with President Obama himself—who not only continued Bush's program of death from the sky but vastly expanded it. In addition to Obama, the list of accused includes the five men who served as his CIA director: Gen. Michael Hayden, Leon Panetta, Michael Morell, David Petraeus and, of course, John Brennan.

Officials and CIA Contractors Responsible for Human Rights Crimes

Name	Position
John Brennan	Director of the National Counterterrorism Center: August 27, 2004–August 1, 2005 United States Homeland Security Advisor: January 20, 2009–March 8, 2013 Director of the Central Intelligence Agency: March 8, 2013–present
George W. Bush	US President: January 20, 2001–January 20, 2009
Dick Cheney	Vice President: January 20, 2001–January 20, 2009

Name	Position
Richard A. Clarke	National Coordinator for Security, Infrastructure Protection, and Counter-terrorism; also Special Advisor to the President on Cybersecurity: 1998–2003
General Michael Hayden (US Air Force, ret.)	Director of the National Security Agency: 1999–2005 Director of National Intelligence: 2005–2006 Director of the Central Intelligence Agency: May 30, 2006–February 12, 2009
Bruce Jessen	US Air Force psychologist leading the Survival, Evasion, Resistance and Escape (SERE) training: before 1988 Principal in Mitchell, Jessen & Associates, contractors to the CIA for interrogation: 2002–April 2009
James Mitchell	US Air Force psychologist leading the Survival, Evasion, Resistance and Escape (SERE) training for part of service: 1988–2001 Principal in Mitchell, Jessen & Associates, contractors to the CIA for interrogation: 2002–April 2009
Michael Morell	Deputy Director of the Central Intelligence Agency: May 6, 2010–August 9, 2013 Acting Director of the Central Intelligence Agency: November 9, 2012–March 8, 2013
Barack Obama	President of the United States: January 20, 2009–present
Leon Panetta	Director of the Central Intelligence Agency: February 13, 2009–June 30, 2011 United States Secretary of Defense: July 1, 2011–February 27, 2013

Name	Position
General David Petraeus	Commander, Multi-National Force—Iraq: February 10, 2007–September 16, 2008 Commander US Central Command: October 31, 2008–June 23, 2010 Commander US and ISAF forces in Afghanistan: July 4, 2010–July 18, 2011 Director of the US CIA: September 6, 2011–November 9, 2012
Donald Rumsfeld	US Secretary of Defense (G W Bush): January 20, 2001–December 18, 2006

Conclusion

American Nuremberg

So, Socrates, injustice, if it is on a large enough scale, is stronger, freer, and more masterly than justice. And, as I said from the first, justice is what is advantageous to the stronger while injustice is to one's own profit and advantage.

> —Thrasymachus, in Plato's *Republic*

The moral arc of the universe is long, but it bends towards justice.

> —Rev. Martin Luther King, Jr. paraphrasing the
> abolitionist Unitarian minister Theodore Parker

To speak of "bringing someone to justice" usually implies a trial, a conviction, and some form of punishment. To speak of justice for the *victims* of crime implies at the very least a public acknowledgement of the harm they have suffered, and the public naming of those responsible for that harm. And it requires—to the extent possible—reparation.

It is extremely unlikely that justice will ever be served if we wait for the US government to punish its own former or current high-ranking officials. Washington will never develop the political will to create its own war crimes tribunal, at least not in my lifetime—that is not the way of imperial capitals. It is always possible that a Dick Cheney or a George Tenet might find himself in the wrong country at the wrong time, a country like Spain or Switzerland that practices universal jurisdiction and is brave enough to indict a former US leader. But our own country, which *should* prosecute our own war criminals, simply will not do it.

If our own government will not do it, and an international tribunal like the one at Nuremberg is not possible, is there any other way to publicly judge these crimes? We need to determine a method that does not simply punish the guilty, but that offers some relief to those who have been victimized and their families. Justice, as Aristotle and St. Aquinas declared, consists in giving people what they are owed. What is owed to the victims of the war on terror and their survivors? What is owed to the system of international law that protects us, however imperfectly, from the depredations of raw military power?

Many of those who work with the victims of organized terror say that the first—the most important—thing is genuine acknowledgement of what has happened to them. This is the deep insight behind the South African Truth and Reconciliation process, the public hearings that sought to exorcise the demons of apartheid—the recognition that there can be no reconciliation without first fully revealing what has been done. In South Africa, those who had tortured and murdered under the apartheid system could receive an amnesty for their crimes, but only after they had publicly acknowledged their actions. It is this acknowledgement of wrong that marks the beginning of justice. As the crime is exposed, the disappeared become visible once more.

Of course, the Truth and Reconciliation process was only possible because it had the official sanction of a new and democratic South African government, one that was under the extraordinary presidency of former revolutionary leader Nelson Mandela. The architect of the Truth and Reconciliation process, Archbishop Desmond Tutu, was another hero of that nation's anti-apartheid resistance movement. The collection of searing stories that were told during this process of national reckoning became part of the official record of the history of a new nation. This was possible because the forces of democracy had triumphed over white rule, and a new government truly had the power to grant or withhold amnesty. Justice in South Africa was, in the best sense of both words, victors' justice. Is there some way this remarkable process could be replicated in the United States, without the support of the federal government?

People's Justice

Those opposed to the war on terror do not, of course, control Congress. We do not have the power to set up official inquiries into war crimes or to offer or withhold an amnesty. We do not have the power to write the official story of this sorry period in US history. In fact, the war we oppose has not even ended. We do not even have the votes in Congress to push for hearings like those convened by Senator Frank Church in 1975, which shed at least some light on the dark actions of the CIA during the Cold War.

But even if we can't hold hearings on Capitol Hill, we must find other ways to honor the victims of the war on terror, as well as the rule of international law. The world demands from the US government a full accounting of all that has happened since 9/11 and a full list of those who are responsible for these dark deeds. As I suggested in the introduction to this book, there are certain concrete steps that Washington could and should take to begin to correct the injustice of our country's vicious war on terror. These are:

1. The United States should permanently end the practice of torture, both in its foreign affairs and in its own jails, prisons, and migrant deportation centers.
2. The United States should pass—and enforce—a federal law that genuinely implements the UN Convention against Torture and Other Cruel, Inhuman or Degrading Treatment or Punishment. The present law only covers crimes occurring *outside* the United States.
3. The United States should join the International Criminal Court, which would make future prosecutions of US citizens possible in an internationally recognized venue.
4. The United States Justice Department should stop resisting torture victims' attempt to sue for damages in US courts. Article 14 of the UN Convention against Torture establishes this obligation: "Each State Party shall ensure in its legal system that the victim of an act of torture obtains redress and has an enforceable right to fair and adequate compensation including the means for as full rehabilitation as possible."
5. The United States should cooperate with, rather than resist, the efforts of other nations to extradite their own accused violators of human rights.

All these measures require US *government* action, action that seems profoundly unlikely in the present political climate. Both mainstream political parties—as well as Congress, the White House and the country's vast military and intelligence machinery—remain committed to a permanent war on terror, whatever name they choose to give it. So what can we do as American citizens?

We can empanel a non-governmental tribunal, a citizens' American Nuremberg. We could do worse than to build on the work of the Constitution Project, which in 2013 published a report indicting "the nation's most senior officials" for torture. Panelists included Republicans and Democrats, former George W. Bush administration officials, a former ambassador, a former head of the FBI, law professors, and a three-star general. The project's focus was limited to the abuse of detainees, but a new panel's charge could be expanded to include all the illegal war-making, the war crimes, and the human rights crimes committed in the war on terror.

There are precedents for such a tribunal. One of the more well-known such citizen efforts was the International War Crimes Tribunal held in Sweden and Denmark in 1967, at the height of the Vietnam War. Near the end of his life, the great British philosopher, mathematician and Nobel Prize winner Bertrand Russell collaborated with the French philosopher Jean Paul Sartre to convene a tribunal on US crimes committed in the Vietnam War. Russell and Sartre drew together a collection of deeply respected literary and political figures, including the writers James Baldwin, Simone de Beauvoir, and Julio Cortázar, as well as Lázaro Cárdenas, a former president of Mexico.

The International War Crimes Tribunal, also known as the Russell Tribunal, considered five questions about the US war in Vietnam:

1. Has the United States Government (and the Governments of Australia, New Zealand and South Korea) committed acts of aggression according to international law?

2. Has the American army made use of or experimented with new weapons or weapons forbidden by the laws of war?

3. Has there been bombardment of targets of a purely civilian character, for example hospitals, schools, sanatoria, dams, etc., and on what scale has this occurred?

4. Have Vietnamese prisoners been subjected to inhuman treatment forbidden by the laws of war and, in particular, to torture or mutilation? Have there been unjustified reprisals against the civilian population, in particular, execution of hostages?

5. Have forced labour camps been created, has there been deportation of the population or other acts tending to the extermination of the population and which can be characterised juridically as acts of genocide?

In arguing for the importance and legitimacy of the Russell Tribunal, Sartre explicitly referred to the precedent set at Nuremberg. "In 1945, something absolutely new in history appeared at Nuremberg with the first international Tribunal formed to pass judgment on crimes committed by a belligerent power," wrote Sartre in his inaugural statement for the Russell Tribunal. Before Nuremberg, the world "continued to operate under the law of the jungle." Nuremberg, stated Sartre, changed that forever.

Tragically, however, Nuremberg left behind no permanent, universally recognized institution that could impose the rule of international law. "Such a body," Sarte believed,

> would not have been difficult to set up. It would have sufficed that the body created for the judgement of the Nazis had continued after its original task, or that the United Nations, considering all the consequences of what had just been achieved, would, by a vote of the General Assembly, have consolidated it into a permanent tribunal, empowered to investigate and to judge all accusations of war crimes, even if the accused should be one of the countries that had been responsible for the sentencing at Nuremberg. In this way, the implicit universality of the original intention would have been clearly defined. However, we know what did happen: hardly had the last guilty German been sentenced than the Tribunal vanished and no one ever heard of it again.

The Nuremberg tribunal might have vanished forever, but it left behind "the embryo of a tradition." And now, Sartre believed, the United States and the allied nations that were wreaking death and destruction in Vietnam could legitimately be tried by the standards set at Nuremberg. But for the Russell Tribunal's organizers, there was something even bigger at stake than judging US war crimes in Vietnam. The tribunal's ultimate purpose was "to make everybody understand the necessity for international jurisdiction," the need for an official international body that could permanently adjudicate the crimes of war, that is, to "resuscitate" the undertaking that was "stillborn at Nuremberg, and to substitute legal, ethical laws for the law of the jungle."

A half century after the Russell Tribunal, such a body still does not exist. The closest approximation we have is the International Criminal Court, but the United States has withdrawn its signature from the treaty that created it. So we find ourselves in the same situation that Russell and Sartre faced in 1967: There is no official international body that has the power to try US war criminals.

Very well. We shall have to create our own tribunal—our own American Nuremberg.

Such an undertaking would require time and careful preparation. It would cost money and require the work of many people. The tribunal's scope would first have to be defined and its procedures agreed upon. Then charges would have to prepared, witnesses located, documents tracked down. Finally, the event would have to be carefully planned and staged to ensure the widest cooperation from across the political spectrum as well as maximum media coverage. But this massive effort would be well worth it. Such a tribunal would both make history and produce a precious historical record.

Such a tribunal might also help resuscitate American democracy. Since the attacks of 9/11, the people of this country have been coached in cowardice, trained to accept any restriction of our liberties—and any criminal action of our government—as the necessary price of an elusive and illusory "security." Facing a supposedly existential enemy, we were told to go shopping. An American Nuremberg might remind us that we are not only consumers but citizens—of this country and of the world.

Recapturing American democracy will take more than a war crimes tribunal. Addressing vast inequalities of race and class and prying the fingers of corporate and plutocratic wealth from the levers of state power are other crucial challenges. But owning up to our own and our government's failures in the war on terror might put us back in the habit of thinking that running our country is *our* business and *our* responsibility.

Even then, there are some things we cannot hope to achieve. American Nuremberg organizers would need to accept the bitter reality that none of the US officials put on "trial" at this tribunal will likely see a day behind bars, even if "convicted" of high crimes. Nor will these war criminals accept the tribunal's jurisdiction or its verdicts. Most of those accused will spend the rest of their lives convinced that what they did during the war on terror was neither torture nor murder, but enhanced interrogation and the swift removal of enemies from the battlefield. They will continue to believe that they made difficult, but legal and righteous, choices for the good of the United States.

Still other warriors against "terror" have no respect for law in any form; theirs is the justice of the philosopher Thrasymachus, who in Plato's *Republic* tells Socrates that "injustice, if it is on a large enough scale, is stronger, freer, and more masterly than justice." These upholders of *realpolitik* believe that justice is no more than the advantage of the strong over the weak, and that anyone who thinks differently is a naïve fool.

Well, then, let us be fools. The world is waiting.

At the first Nuremberg tribunal, twenty-two Nazi officials and collaborators stood trial. Here is a list of the twenty-two most egregious criminals of the war on terror:

Name	Position
David Addington	Minority Counsel to the House-Senate Committee investigating Iran-Contra: 1987 Chief Counsel to US Vice-President: 2001–2005 Chief of Staff to US Vice President: November 1, 2005–January 20, 2009
Steven Bradbury	Principal Deputy Assistant Attorney General for Office of Legal Counsel of the Department of Justice: April 2004 Acting Assistant Attorney General for Office of Legal Counsel: though never confirmed by Senate, 2005–2009
John Brennan	Director of the National Counterterrorism Center: August 27, 2004–August 1, 2005 United States Homeland Security Advisor: January 20, 2009–March 8, 2013 Director of the Central Intelligence Agency: March 8, 2013–present
George W. Bush	US President: January 20, 2001–January 20, 2009
Jay Bybee	Assistant Attorney General, Office of Legal Counsel of the Department of Justice: January 2001–March 13, 2003
Stephen Cambone	Under Secretary of Defense for Intelligence: March 7, 2003–December 31, 2006
Dick Cheney	Vice President: January 20, 2001–January 20, 2009
Michael D'Andrea	Chief of Operations and Director, CIA Counterterrorism Center: 2001-2015

Name	Position
Gen. Michael Hayden (US Air Force, ret.)	Director of the National Security Agency: 1999–2005 Director of National Intelligence: 2005–2006 Director of the Central Intelligence Agency: May 30, 2006–February 12, 2009
William J. "Jim" Haynes	General Counsel of the Department of Defense: May 24, 2001–March 10, 2008
Bruce Jessen	US Air Force psychologist leading the Survival, Evasion, Resistance and Escape (SERE) training: before 1988 Principal in Mitchell, Jessen & Associates, contractors to the CIA for interrogation: 2002–April 2009
Gen. Stanley McChrystal	Commander, Joint Special Operations Command: 2003–2008 Commander, International Security Assistance Force (ISAF) and Commander, US Forces Afghanistan (USFOR-A): June 15, 2009–June 23, 2010
Major Gen. Geoffrey Miller	Commander of US detention facilities at Guantánamo Bay, Cuba and in Iraq: November 2002–November 2004
James Mitchell	US Air Force psychologist leading the Survival, Evasion, Resistance and Escape (SERE) training for part of service: 1988–2001 Principal in Mitchell, Jessen & Associates, contractors to the CIA for interrogation: 2002–April 2009
John Negroponte	US Ambassador to the United Nations (G.W. Bush): September 15, 2001–April 2004 US Ambassador to Iraq: May 6, 2004–April 2005 US Director of National Intelligence: April 21, 2005–February 13, 2007 US Deputy Secretary of State: February 13, 2007–January 20, 2009

Name	Position
Barack Obama	President of the United States: January 20, 2009–present
Gen. David Petraeus	Commander, Multi-National Force—Iraq: February 10, 2007–September 16, 2008 Commander US Central Command: October 31, 2008–June 23, 2010 Commander US and ISAF forces in Afghanistan: July 4, 2010–July 18, 2011 Director of the US CIA: September 6, 2011–November 9, 2012
Condoleezza Rice	US National Security Advisor: January 20, 2001–January 26, 2005 US Secretary of State: January 26, 2005–January 20, 2009
John Rizzo	Acting General Counsel of the CIA: November 2001–2002 Deputy General Counsel: 2002–2004; Acting General Counsel of the CIA: again mid-2004–October 2009
Donald Rumsfeld	US Secretary of Defense (G W Bush): January 20, 2001–December 18, 2006
Paul Wolfowitz	US Deputy Secretary of Defense: January 20, 2001–June 1, 2005
John Yoo	Deputy Assistant Attorney General, Office of Legal Counsel, US Department of Justice: 2001–2003

BIBLIOGRAPHY

Associated Press. (2005, June 5). Bolton Linked to Firing of U.N. Arms Monitor. *Los Angeles Times*. Retrieved from http://articles.latimes.com/2005/jun/05/nation/na-bolton5

Breyer, Stephen. (2006). *Concurring opinion, Hamdan v. Rumsfeld (No. 05-184)* Retrieved from https://www.law.cornell.edu/supct/html/05-184.ZC.html.

Brown, DeNeen L., & Priest, Dana. (2003, November 5). Deported Terror Suspect Details Torture in Syria; Canadian's Case Called Typical of C.I.A. *Washington Post*. Retrieved from http://pqasb.pqarchiver.com/washingtonpost/access/437588671.html?dids=437588671:437588671&FMT=ABS&FMTS=ABS:FT&date=Nov+5%2C+2003&author=DeNeen+L.+Brown+and+Dana+Priest&pub=The+Washington+Post&edition=&startpage=A.01&desc=Deported+Terror+Suspect+Details+Torture+in+Syria

Bush, George W. (2001). President Bush Addresses the Nation.

Bush, George W. (2002a). *Humane Treatment of al Qaeda and Taliban Detainees.* Washington, DC Retrieved from http://www.washington-post.com/wp-srv/nation/documents/020702bush.pdf.

Bush, George W. (2002b). Transcript of Speech to the Nation: CNN.

Bush, George W. (2010). *Decision Points* (1st ed.). New York: Crown Publishers.

Bybee, Jay S. (2002). *Memorandum for Alberto R. Gonzales, Counsel to the President Re: Standards of Conduct for Interrogation under 18 U.S.C. 2340-2340A*: U.S, Department of Justice.

Calvocoressi, Peter. (1947). *Nuremberg: The Facts the Law and the Consequences.* London: Chatto and Windus.

Cheney, Richard B., & Cheney, Liz. (2011). *In My Time : A Personal and Political Memoir.* New York: Threshold Editions.

Conot, Robert E. (1983). *Justice at Nuremberg* (1st ed.). New York: Harper & Row.

Davidson, Amy. (2012). Torturing the Wrong Man. *The New Yorker.* Retrieved from Close Read website: http://www.newyorker.com/online/blogs/closeread/2012/12/khaled-el-masri-torturing-the-wrong-man.html Retrieved from http://www.newyorker.com/online/blogs/closeread/2012/12/khaled-el-masri-torturing-the-wrong-man.html

Department of Defense. (2003). Wolfowitz Interview with Vanity Fair's Tannenhaus. In Sam Tannenhaus (Ed.).

Emmerson, Ben, UN Special Rapporteur on Counter-Terrorism and Human Rights. (2013). *Promotion and protection of human rights and fundamental freedoms while countering terrorism* Retrieved from http://msnbcmedia.msn.com/i/msnbc/sections/news/UN_Drones_Report.pdf

Gall, Carlotta. (2003, March 4). U.S. Military Investigating Death of Afghan in Custody. *New York Times.* Retrieved from http://www.nytimes.com/2003/03/04/international/asia/04AFGH.html?pagewanted=all

Governments of United States of America, United Kingdom, the Soviet Union, and China,. (1943). Joint Four-Nation Declaration. Moscow.

International Committee of the Red Cross. (2010a). Challenges for IHL - terrorism: overview. Retrieved from ICRC - War and Law, Contemporary Challenges website: https://www.icrc.org/eng/war-and-law/contemporary-challenges-for-ihl/terrorism/overview-terrorism.htm Retrieved from https://www.icrc.org/eng/war-and-law/contemporary-challenges-for-ihl/terrorism/overview-terrorism.htm

International Committee of the Red Cross. (2010b). Founding and early years of the ICRC (1863-1914).

International Law Commission. (1950). Principles of International Law recognized in the Charter of the Nürnberg Tribunal and in the Judgment of the Tribunal, with commentaries United Nations.

Jackson, Rohert H. (1945). Opening Statement, Nuermberg Trials. Nuremberg, Germany.

Jehl, Douglas. (2005, December 9). Qaeda-Iraq Link U.S. Cited Is Tied to Coercion Claim *New York Times*. Retrieved from http://www.nytimes.com/2005/12/09/politics/09intel.html

Obama, Barack. (2014). Press Conference by the President. Washington.

Project Censored. (2010). Secrets of Cheney's Energy Task Force Come to Light. http://www.projectcensored.org/8-secrets-of-cheneys-energy-task-force-come-to-light/ Retrieved from http://www.projectcensored.org/8-secrets-of-cheneys-energy-task-force-come-to-light/

Richard Perle et al. (1998). Letter to President Clinton on Iraq. http://www.rightweb.irc-online.org/images/uploads/PNAC_Letter_to_President_Clinton_on_Iraq.pdf Retrieved from http://www.rightweb.irc-online.org/images/uploads/PNAC_Letter_to_President_Clinton_on_Iraq.pdf

Rohde, David. (2015). Exclusive: Detainee alleges CIA sexual abuse, torture beyond Senate findings. *Reuters*. Reutershttp://www.reuters.com/

article/2015/06/02/us-usa-torture-khan-idUSKBN0OI1TW2015 0602#lcOmiRkwqiko1Ys3.99 Retrieved from Reutershttp://www. reuters.com/article/2015/06/02/us-usa-torture-khan-idUSKB N0OI1TW20150602#lcOmiRkwqiko1Ys3.99

Rumsfeld, Donald. (2001, September 23) /*Interviewer: Bob Schieffer*. CBS Face the Nation.

Rumsfeld, Donald. (2002). *Secretary Rumsfeld Statement on the ICC Treaty*. Washington, DC Retrieved from http://www.amicc.org/docs/Rumsfeld5_6_02.pdf.

Sassòli, Marco. (2006). Transnational Armed Groups and International Humanitarian Law. *Harvard Program on Humanitarian Law and Conflict Research, Occasional Papers Series*. http://www.hpcrresearch.org/sites/default/files/publications/OccasionalPaper6.pdf Retrieved from http://www.hpcrresearch.org/sites/default/files/publications/OccasionalPaper6.pdf

Scahill, Jeremy. (2013). *Dirty Wars: The World is a Battlefield* (First edition. ed.). New York: Nation Books.

Schell, Jonathan. (2003, March 27). The Other Superpower. *The Nation*.

Schulberg, Jessica. (2014). The Forever War Was Supposed to End in 2014. Instead, Obama Doubled Down. *The New Republic*. Retrieved from newrepublic.com website: http://www.newrepublic.com/article/120643/isis-made-obama-continue-war-terror-new-aumf Retrieved from http://www.newrepublic.com/article/120643/isis-made-obama-continue-war-terror-new-aumf

Slahi, Mohamedou Ould, & Siems, Larry. (2015). *Guantánamo diary* (First edition. ed.). New York: Little, Brown and Company.

Taylor, Telford. (2013). *The Anatomy of the Nuremberg trials : a personal memoir*. New York: Skyhorse Publishing.

The Constitution Project. (2013). *The Report of The Constitution Project's Task Force on Detainee Treatment*. Washington: The Constitution Project.

Unger, Craig. (2006, July). The War They Wanted, the Lies They Needed. *Vanity Fair*.

Vesser, Dale A., Khalilzad, Zalmay M., & Wolfowitz, Paul. (1992). *Defense Position Guidance*. Washington Retrieved from http://www.archives. gov/declassification/iscap/pdf/2008-003-docs1-12.pdf.

Worthington, Andy. (2007). *The Guantánamo files: the stories of the 774 detainees in America's illegal prison*. Ann Arbor: Pluto Press.

ENDNOTES

Introduction

Chapter 1

Chapter 2

Chapter 3

72   *"The perceived capability of the US to act independently . . . "* (Vesser, Khalilzad, & Wolfowitz, 1992)

71   *The* Los Angeles Times *credited Bolton . . .* (Associated Press, 2005)

75   *Cheney convened the National Energy Policy Development Group . . .* (Project Censored, 2010)

77   *The forged documents were full of errors . . .* (Unger, 2006)

79   *Cheney's memoir also uses the phrase . . .* (Cheney & Cheney, 2011)

87   *as Paul Wolfowitz later told* Vanity Fair *. . .* (Department of Defense, 2003)

89   *A new phenomenon of rolling demonstrations . . .* (Schell, 2003)

Chapter 4

99   *"When a president of the United States want[s] . . . "* (Scahill, 2013)

100   *" the ICC provisions claim the authority to detain and try American citizens . . . "* (Rumsfeld, 2002)

103   *"[p]ulmonary embolism due to blunt force injury to the legs . . . "* (Gall, 2003)

103   *"together with an unknown number of fleeing civilians . . . "* (The Constitution Project, 2013)

105   *and renders quaint some of its provisions . . . "* (Office of Legal Counsel, 2002)

105   "[a] White House lawyer with direct knowledge . . . " (Gellman, 2007)

107   *Muller issued a memorandum "for the record . . . "* (Muller, 2003)

113   *Bradbury gave Rizzo the answer he was hoping for* (Bradbury, 2005)

113   *In September 2006, in a televised address, Bush acknowledged* (BBC News, 2007)

114   *He justified his veto by saying . . .* (Bush, 2008)

116 *"We're not going to read more people than necessary into our heart of darkness."* (Hersh, 2004)

117 *As early as December 2002, stories about what went on in them began to surface* (Priest, 2005)

118 *"Even the closest of allies differ over tactics and strategy . . . "* (Tenet, 2002)

120 His name did not become public until April 2015 . . . (Mazzetti, 2015)

121 *The suggested methods included confinement in small spaces . . .* (Bybee, 2002)

125 *"There was sadism on the night shift at Abu Ghraib . . . "* (CNN, 2004)

125 *Major General Antonio Taguba's report on Abu Ghraib . . .* (Taguba, 2004)

128 *"They put his body in a body bag . . . "* (Frederick II, 2003)

131 *Jim Haynes . . . sent a memo to Rumsfeld . . .* (Haynes II, 2002)

132 *"While methods employed at Abu Ghraib . . . "* (White, 2005)

136 *"Unlike covert actions undertaken by the CIA . . . "* (Mazzetti, 2010)

137 *"Every single detention centre would have its own interrogation committee . . . "* (Mahmood, 2013)

139 *a story about a documentary produced by a state-run Italian news channel* (Burns, 2005) The video is available at http://www.rain-ews.it/ran24/inchiesta/video.asp

129 *Saddam Saleh Aboud spoke to New York Times reporter Ian Fisher . . .* (Fisher, 2004)

Chapter 5

143 "We don't kick the shit out of them . . . " (Priest, 2002)

143 *"If you are going to murder someone . . . "* (Scahill, 2013)

144 *When the CIA kidnapped Abd al-Rahim al-Nashiri in Dubai . . .* (Senate Select Committee on Intelligence, 2014)

146 *"That's a no brainer. Of course it's a violation of international law . . . "* (Clarke, 2004)

147 *". . . weren't worth a bucket of warm spit."* (Mayer, 2008)

148 *Slahi used his fourth or fifth language . . .* (Slahi, 2015)

148 *"he was tortured for months with electric shocks . . . "* (Whitlock, 2006)

149 *"chapter in the . . . intelligence–psychological warfare–information war . . . "* (D'Avanzo, 2010)

151 *. . . the CIA continues to run at least one interrogation center . . .* (Scahill, 2011)

152 *Bybee's memo reminded Rizzo . . .* (Bybee, 2002)

153 *" he helped smuggle Al Qaida leaders out of Afghanistan . . . "* (Bush, 2006)

158 *Hasan Moqbel described the procedure . . .* (Moqbel, 2013)

160 *"Careful records are kept of each interrogation . . . "* (Bradbury, 2005)

161 *"It felt like they were experimenting . . . "* See the Rendition Project at http://www.therenditionproject.org.uk/prisoners/zubaydah.html

163 *In fact, a 2004 CIA document from the agency's own Inspector General's office . . .* (CIA Office of Inspector General, 2004)

165 *President Obama publicly announced a shift . . .* (Obama, 2013)

165 *Arafat Qa'id Salem Arfaj and his three brothers . . .* (Singh, 2015)

167 *forty-eight drone strikes in Pakistan between 2004 and 2008 . . .* (NewAmerica Foundation, 2015)

167 *In Pakistan, over sixty percent of all strikes target domestic buildings . . .* (Ross, 2014)

168 *In a paper dated November 8, 2011 . . .* (Isikoff, 2013)

170 *In his 2013 report to the UN General Assembly . . .* (Heyns, 2013)

172 *An April 15, 2015, Wall Street Journal story . . .* (Entous, 2015)

172 *The "signature" can be as ill-defined as . . .* (Ackerman, 2015)

172 *"When the C.I.A. sees 'three guys doing jumping jacks . . . .'"* (Becker, 2012)

Conclusion

Index

Aboud, Saddam Saleh, 129–31
Abrams, Eliot, 70, 95
Abu Ghraib prison, 3, 103, 124–
 25, 140. *See also* Abu Ghraib
 torture
Abu Ghraib torture, 124–27,
 129–31; damage control over,
 125–28; exposure of, 3, 124,
 133–34; goals of, 128–29;
 responsibility for, 126, 127,
 131–33
Addington, David, 105, 109,
 110–11, 116, 140, 188
Afghanistan, 28, 71–72, 100, 152.
 See also Afghanistan War
Afghanistan War (2001—), 8, 10,
 86–87, 98, 136, 148; ambiguous
 legality of, 66; Barack Obama
 and, 35, 36; Congress and, 35;
 estimated casualties in, 82, 174;

and Geneva Conventions, 34,
 36–37, 43–45, 99–100, 104–6,
 107, 118–19
—prisoner abuse in, 99–100,
 101–4, 114–21, 126, 143–44;
 high-level approval of, 104–14,
 116, 117; psychologists and,
 121–23
al-Awlaki, Anwar, 168, 169, 171
al-Dossari, Juma, 115
Alexander, Michelle, 13
al-Harethi, Salim Sinan, 167, 168
al-Hawsawi, Mustafa, 120
al-Jamadi, Manadel, 127–28
al-Libi, Ibn al-Shaykh, 62–63, 151
al-Najjar, Ridha, 119
al-Nashiri, Abd al-Rahim, 120,
 144
al Qaeda, 27, 34–35, 62, 105, 159;
 attempts to link, with Iraq, 3,

Church, Frank, 181; 1975 hearings held by (Church Commission), 162, 181
Churchill, Winston, 6, 17
Clarke, Richard E., 145–46, 176
Clinton, Bill, 50, 69, 72, 73, 142, 145–47
Clinton, Hillary Rodham, 90
cluster bombs, 39, 65, 138
COBALT site. *See* "Salt Pit," the
Coffman, James H., 137, 141
Cold War, 5, 7, 16, 17–18, 73, 77; CIA and, 123–24, 145, 162, 181
confinement: in small spaces, 121, 154; solitary, 47, 158
conspiracy charges, 24
Constitution Project, 103–4, 183
contractors. *See* private contractors
Convention against Torture and Other Cruel, Inhuman, or Degrading Treatment or Punishment (UN Convention against Torture, CAT), 47, 51–54, 55, 59, 182; embodiment of, in US law, 51, 144 (*see also* US Code 2340); US ratification of 49–50, 51; violations of, 51–52, 53–54, 144, 149–51, 160–61
"Copper Green" ("Matchbox") program, 116–17
Cortázar, Julio, 183
"crimes against humanity" (term), 10–11, 21, 23
Cruz, Ted, 175
Cutler, Lloyd, 146

Dailey, Dell L., 104, 141
D'Andrea, Michael, 120, 140, 188

Daniels, Deborah J., 109
Darby, Joe, 133–34
"Dark Prison," the. *See* "Salt Pit," the
Dark Side, The (Mayer), 146–47
"dark sites" (CIA secret prisons), 3, 46n, 52, 144, 145, 154, 159
Davidson, Amy, 46n
de Beauvoir, Simone, 183
Decision Points (Bush), 79, 86, 157
Defense Intelligence Agency (DIA), 78, 98, 101, 143
"Defense Planning Guidance" document (DPG, 1992), 72–73
Derwish, Kamal, 167
Detainee Treatment Act (2006), 47–49, 58
Diego Garcia, 151
Dilawar, 28, 102–3
DiNenna, David, 132
"directing hands," 19
Dirty Wars (Scahill), 99, 116
Dobriansky, Paula, 70
dogs, 130, 131, 132–33
Dostum, Abdul Rashid, 103
drone assassinations, 3, 29, 120, 164–75; Barack Obama and, 145, 164–65, 167, 168, 172, 173–74, 175; civilian deaths in, 164–66, 167–68, 172–73, 174; in Pakistan, 164, 167–68, 171, 172, 174; weak justifications for, 168–72
Dulles, Allen, 123
Dunant, Henry, 39–40
Dunbar, Robin, 65

Egypt, 62, 102, 118, 119, 146–47, 148, 149–50
Eichmann, Adolf, 5–6

El Salvador, 137
El-Masri, Khalid, 45–46
Emmanuel, Charles McArthur, 55
Emmerson, Ben, 1
England, Lynndie, 129
Esquire magazine, 135
Executive Order 12333 (Carter), 162, 169
Executive Order 13440 (G. W. Bush), 34
ex post facto laws, 22, 24, 26
extradition, 98, 146, 147, 148, 149, 182
extrajudicial killing, 37, 98, 145, 165, 170–71. *See also* drone assassinations
"extraordinary rendition," 3, 10, 29, 51–52, 102, 145–51; CIA and, 3, 62–63, 144, 145, 146, 147–51; nations cooperating in, 52, 62, 102, 118, 119, 146–47, 148, 149–50; as violation of international law, 51-52, 145–46, 149

Fallujah, 82–83, 138–39
Federal Bureau of Investigation (FBI), 2, 115–16, 183
Feith, Douglas, 68, 73, 95, 131, 141
force feedings, 158–59
Ford, Gerald, 162
Foreign Affairs Reform and Restructuring Act (1998), 149
Foust, Joshua, 143
Franks, Tommy, 82, 104
Frederick, Ivan, II, 126, 128
Fritzsche, Hans, 26
Fukuyama, Francis, 70

Gall, Carlotta, 103

Gehlen, Reinhard, 90n
Gellman, Barton, 117, 150
Geneva Conventions, 7, 22, 23, 57, 114, 171; Additional Protocols of, 32, 41–42; and Afghanistan War, 34, 36–37, 43–45, 99–100, 104–6, 107, 118–19; Common Article 3 of, 40, 41, 42, 46, 47, 48–49, 101, 105, 106; and Iraq War, 125–26, 134; and meaning of "armed conflict," 32, 36, 46; origins of, 39–40; role accorded in, to Red Cross, 32, 33; US efforts to redefine, 33–34, 44–45, 104–6, 107, 109, 116, 121; violations of, as war crimes, 98, 100, 163
—and US law: and 1996 Military Commissions Act, 41; and 1996 War Crimes Act, 100–101, 138, 159–60; and US Constitution, 34, 46
genocide treaty (1948), 23
"ghost prisoners," 3, 45, 127–28
Globke, Hans, 90n
Goebbels, Joseph, 5
Goering, Hermann, 5, 18, 25n
Gonzales, Alberto R., 108, 109, 110, 112, 141; on Geneva Conventions, 40–41, 105
Gordon, Michael R., 80
Gore, Al, 146
Graner, Charles, 129, 133
Grey, Stephen, 149
Grotius, Hugo, 22–23
Guantánamo Diary (Slahi), 147–48
Guantánamo Files, The (Worthington), 114, 147, 150–51